# THE STAY BEHINDS

OSPREY
PUBLISHING

For August and Ingmar

# THE STAY BEHINDS

## SWEDEN'S COLD WAR GUARDIANS

JOHAN WENNSTRÖM

Translated by Stephen Donovan

OSPREY PUBLISHING
Bloomsbury Publishing Plc
Kemp House, Chawley Park, Cumnor Hill, Oxford OX2 9PH, UK
Bloomsbury Publishing Ireland Limited,
29 Earlsfort Terrace, Dublin 2, D02 AY28, Ireland
Bloomsbury Publishing Inc.
1359 Broadway, 12th Floor, New York, NY 10018, USA
E-mail: info@ospreypublishing.com
www.ospreypublishing.com

OSPREY is a trademark of Osprey Publishing Ltd

First published in Great Britain in 2026



A catalogue record for this book is available from the British Library.

ISBN: HB 9781472877543; eBook 9781472877567; ePDF 9781472877574; XML 9781472877581; Audio 9781472877598

26 27 28 29 30 10 9 8 7 6 5 4 3 2 1

Index by Kate Inskip

Typeset by Lumina Datamatics Ltd
Printed and bound in Great Britain by Clays Ltd, Elcograf S.p.A.

MIX
Paper | Supporting responsible forestry
FSC® C018072
FSC www.fsc.org

# Contents

# Foreword

"They also serve who only stand and wait," wrote John Milton in his *Sonnet 19*. It is possible to be a genuine hero of Freedom and Democracy without having had to fight in a war. To stand ready, perhaps for decades, to train, learn very special skills, and to be prepared to place yourself in mortal danger if your country is invaded; that is heroic whether the invasion comes or not.

The Stay Behind operatives so superbly evoked in this well-researched, well-written and intellectually groundbreaking book, finally have a fitting memorial to their steadfastness in the face of what President Reagan correctly called an "evil Empire".

Marxism-Leninism in general, and Soviet communism in particular, is an inherently expansionist ideology. It saw the dictatorship of the proletariat as its ultimate global goal, requiring the unanimity of the planet fully to enact that warped ideal. Every chance that the USSR had to thrust its creed onto foreign countries, it took. Patriotic Swedes such as Tage Erlander and Alvar Lindencrona were therefore extremely far-sighted in setting up a secret organization that would operate far behind enemy lines should there be a successful Soviet invasion of Sweden.

We can see from the incredibly vicious Soviet invasions of Poland in 1920 and 1939, Finland in 1939, Latvia, Lithuania and Estonia in 1940, Hungary in 1956, Czechoslovakia in 1968,

Afghanistan in 1979 and now Ukraine on 24 February 2022, how horrifically harsh a Russian occupation of Sweden would have been if the Cold War had turned boiling hot. The small Swedish Army would have fought valiantly, but it could not have held back a Red Army that numbered over five million troops.

There are revisionist historians today who claim that the Russians were only ever acting defensively against an imperialist NATO during the Cold War, but in that case, why did they spend the 1970s seeking to destabilize democratic regimes in Asia, Africa and South America? Why did they maintain a vast tank force in Eastern Europe, far larger than that of NATO? The truth was that they were always looking for opportunities for expansion, and it was thanks to the resilience and vigilance of the West that they were not given any.

If the Soviet Union had invaded and occupied Sweden, it would have been up to the heroic Stay Behinds to continue resisting them, long after Russian propaganda started telling Swedes that all further defiance was futile. From all classes and ages and backgrounds and occupations, the Stay Behinds would have used their training to carry out acts of sabotage that would have held back significant numbers of Red Army troops behind their front lines, and shown to the world that the Swedes were far from the neutral pacifists that their detractors sometimes portrayed them to be.

We can be certain that the Russian response, led by the KGB and GRU (Russian Military Intelligence), would have been utterly brutal, and would undoubtedly have extended to torture and mass reprisals against civilians. In 1940, the NKVD, the forerunner of the KGB, shot 14,000 Polish officers in the Katyn Forest, and tried (ultimately unsuccessfully) to blame it on the Nazis. It would have taken iron nerves – of the kind that Alvar Lindencrona, the Stay Behind commander, and his colleagues undoubtedly possessed – not to have crumbled in the face of Soviet repression.

In May 2023, I visited Bucha and Irpin in Ukraine, and saw the site of a mass grave where the Russians had buried 116 corpses of innocent people they had massacred in cold blood. Sweden would undoubtedly have suffered the same horrors if she had been invaded.

The original template for Stay Behind organizations was the (deliberately opaquely named) "Auxiliary Units" set up by General Colin Gubbins when Britain was under threat of invasion by the Nazis in 1940. There had of course been guerrilla fighters many times before in history – the Spanish and Portuguese partisans in the Peninsular War, for example – but Gubbins was the first person to set up a resistance organization before an invasion took place. He identified prominent, strong-willed, trustworthy people in their communities and trained them in sabotage, radio transmission, explosives, secret inks, martial arts, forgery, and how to survive in the open countryside.

Auxiliary Units typically comprised six or seven men, who were supported by "secret duties personnel" (civilian spies). They were to provide the core for a post-invasion British resistance movement. Their underground hideouts, called "OBs", sometimes had 200ft-long escape tunnels. They were well camouflaged and were only ever visited at night, so that civilians did not stumble upon them. Each had a lookout hidden outside, with a phone connection to the OB. Some were corrugated iron shelters hidden underground – one was under a cucumber frame in the orchard of a Hampshire manor house – and they served as supply dumps for sub-machine guns and explosives.

The Units might not have been able seriously to disrupt Nazi control, but as Colonel J. Wedgwood, one of their commanders, later put it: "The true purpose of resistance is to preserve a nation's soul." Typically they were made up of farmers, gamekeepers (who were considered "very useful"), veterans and students. Another commander, Major John Forbes, recalled one of his operatives as, "A very good man, ruthless, a butcher who wouldn't have minded slitting throats at all." The recruits were generally quite young, few were over 40, and were spread across almost the entire country.

When I interviewed Colonel Sir Douglas Dodds-Parker, a senior member of General Gubbins' staff, for my first book in 1988, I asked him how long British resistance might have lasted against a Nazi invasion. He thought for a moment, before replying, "Greek resistance against Ottoman rule lasted six hundred years."

As well as the Auxiliary Units, another strong inspiration for the Stay Behinds was the Norwegian Linge underground resistance organization that struck the Nazis' nuclear heavy water programme at Telemark in Operations *Grouse*, *Freshman* and *Gunnerside* during World War II. There can be no doubt that if the Cold War had turned into World War III – which it easily could have on several occasions, such as during the Cuban Missile Crisis – the Stay Behinds would have shown similarly remarkable heroism in the face of a different, but similar, totalitarian dictatorship. That is why Stay Behind commanders such as Curt-Steffan Giesecke should be much honoured today, both in his native Sweden and beyond.

Yet it was not all excitement and derring-do; the distinguished scholar Dr Wennström does not shy away from describing the very real human cost on the Stay Behinds of spending lives in the shadows, not being able to tell anyone – even close family – about the contribution they were making to national security. This book will hopefully allow the families of Stay Behinds to recognize what important service their loved ones rendered to the cause of Freedom, even if they could not know about it at the time.

Dr Wennström, as well as the historian Magnus Hjort, have done a fine job of exploding various myths and conspiracy theories about the Stay Behinds, some of which sound as though they might well have originally emanated from the Kremlin's propaganda department. The Stay Behinds were not a shady, right-wing elitist band, for example, nor were they acting beyond normal democratic constraints, and they were certainly not coordinated by the CIA. Instead, they were a properly constituted, independent secret force that served its country well, and almost certainly acted as a deterrence against a Russian invasion, because no regular army wants to "swallow the porcupine" and have to face guerrilla activity operating along its lines of communication.

The obvious reason why the Stay Behinds' training and activities had to be kept out of the Swedish press was the perfectly reasonable one that they had to stay completely undercover, to protect their efficacy in the event of war. When, for example, Dr Wennström praises Swedish Prime Minister Tage Erlander for doing "what was necessary first, and then what was appropriate", all objective readers will wholeheartedly agree.

Because of its very nature as a secret organization, the Stay Behinds were an extremely difficult subject to research, but Dr Wennström's work in a wide range of sources, especially interviews but also in plenty of unpublished documents, means that this book is unlikely to be superseded, but will remain for decades the standard work on the subject, extremely useful to specialist researchers and the general reader alike.

This book could also not be more timely. As we know from the published writings of General Vasily Gerasimov, Vladimir Putin's Chief of Staff, Russia's military doctrine is based on hybrid warfare, covering every aspect of aggressive operations, both overt and covert. The "Gerasimov Doctrine", as it is known, has been focussed against Sweden even more heavily since March 2024, when that country took the statesmanlike step of joining NATO in response to Russia's monstrous, unprovoked and opportunistic attack on Ukraine. Swedes would do well to read this book, and see how their brave forefathers readied themselves against Russian aggression in the past, as all the signs suggest that the West faces a similarly evil empire today.

"All of us were utterly committed to the task," the hotelier Reinhold Geijer recalled of his service as a Swedish Stay Behind, "and felt that we were doing a service for our country." This highly readable book, the product of a huge amount of meticulous research in brand new sources, proves beyond doubt that Mr Geijer was correct.

Lord Roberts of Belgravia<br>House of Lords, London<br>December 2025

# *Dramatis Personae*

Selected qualifications. Period of appointment given when known.

**Richard Åkerman** (1898–1981): Chief of the Defence Staff 1951–57.

**Carl Eric Almgren** (1913–2001): divisional head, Defence Staff 1953–57; Chief of the Defence Staff 1961–67; military commander, Eastern Military District 1967–69; Chief of the Army 1969–76.

**Sven Andersson** (1910–87): Minister of Defence (Social Democratic Party) 1957–73; Minister of Foreign Affairs 1973–76.

**Elov Bergkvist** (1907–99): director, Thule 1947–55; CEO, Fylgia 1955–65; CEO, Trygg-Fylgia 1965–71; deputy chairman, Trygg-Hansa 1971–77; operations director of the resistance organization 1949–66.

**Carl Bildt** (1949–): Prime Minister (Moderate Party) 1991–94.

**Anders E. Bjelle** (1894–1961): CEO, Lantbruksförbundets tidskriftsaktiebolag (LT) 1934–61; deputy chairman, Norgehjälpen 1942–45; member of the Defence Commission 1945–47; deputy chairman, Europahjälpen 1946–50; member of the Volunteer Commission 1948–50; board member of the resistance organization 1949–61.

**Anders Björck** (1944–): Minister of Defence (Moderate Party) 1991–94.

**Carl XVI Gustaf** (1946–): Crown Prince of Sweden 1947–73; King 1973–.

**Ingvar Carlsson** (1934–): political secretary, Prime Minister's Office (Social Democratic Party) 1958–60; chairman, Swedish Social Democratic Youth League (SSU) 1961–67; Prime Minister 1986–91 and 1994–96.

**Lars Carlsson** (1876–1965): harbourmaster in Grundsund 1924–48; maternal grandfather of Lennart Grundborn; friend of Alvar Lindencrona and Gustaf Lindencrona, Sr.

**Roine Carlsson** (1937–2020): Minister of Defence (Social Democratic Party) 1985–91.

**William Colby** (1920–96): CIA officer at the American Embassy in Stockholm 1951–53; director, CIA 1973–76.

**Carl August Ehrensvärd** (1892–1974): chief of staff, Swedish Volunteer Corps 1939–40; Chief of the Defence Staff 1945–47; Chief of the Army 1948–57; board member of the resistance organization 1949–51.

**Birger Elmér** (1919–99): chief, B Bureau 1957–65; IB 1965–75.

**Björn Eriksson** (1945–): chief, Swedish Customs Service and Coastguard 1983–88; National Police Commissioner 1988–96; president, Interpol 1994–96; Governor of Östergötland 1996–2009; board member of the resistance organization.

**Tage Erlander** (1901–85): State Secretary, Ministry of Social Affairs (Social Democratic Party) 1938–44, Deputy Minister 1944–45; Prime Minister 1946–69.

**Thorbjörn Fälldin** (1926–2016): Prime Minister (Centre Party) 1976–82.

**Arne Geijer** (1910–79): education ombudsman, Swedish Metal Workers' Union 1938–45, secretary 1945–48, chairman 1948–56; member of parliament (Social Democratic Party) 1955–76; chairman, Swedish Trade Union Confederation (LO) 1956–73; board member of the resistance organization 1950–73.

**Reinhold "Regi" Geijer** (1917–2009): officer, Svea Life Guards (L1) 1942–55; managing director, Storliens högfjällshotell 1955–79; managing director, Sällskapet 1980–90; regional chief in the resistance organization 1957–69.

**Curt-Steffan Giesecke** (1921–2016): Bachelor of Laws; secretary, Swedish Employers' Confederation (SAF) 1947–54, deputy director 1954–66, director 1966–78; CEO, Trygg-Hansa 1978–86; board member of the resistance organization 1966–78, commander 1978–95.

**Anders Grafström** (1909–79): second lieutenant, Norrland Dragoon Regiment (K4) 1931–33; leader of company in the Swedish volunteer forces 1939–41; adjutant to Carl August Ehrensvärd 1948–52; deputy commander, Svea Life Guards (L1) 1952–55; defence attaché in Helsinki 1955–58; chief, Military Academy Karlberg 1958–64; temporary military commander, Military District II 1964–66; army inspector, Southern Military District 1966–67; operations director of the resistance organization.

**Lennart Grundborn** (1931–2020): author; employee, Thule 1952–64; grandson of Lars Carlsson.

**Gustaf V** (1872–1950): Crown Prince of Sweden 1872–1907, King 1907–50.

**Gustaf VI Adolf** (1907–73): Crown Prince of Sweden 1907–50, King 1950–73.

**Otto Hallberg** (1908–68): chairman, Swedish National Socialist Party's student association in Stockholm; foreign contributor, *Aftonbladet* 1939–40; volunteer soldier, Continuation War 1941; leader of Sveaborg.

**Per Albin Hansson** (1885–1946): Prime Minister (Social Democratic Party) 1932–36 and 1936–46.

**Åke Hasselrot** (1909–97): Bachelor of Laws; chief superintendent, Swedish Security Service 1948–64; deputy police commissioner, Stockholm Police 1965–74; legal advisor to the resistance organization.

**Gunnar Hedlund** (1900–89): Minister of the Interior (Farmers' League) 1951–57.

**Rune Johansson** (1915–82): baker; Minister of the Interior (Social Democratic Party) 1957–62.

**Bertil Jonsson** (1940–): deputy chairman, Swedish Trade Union Confederation (LO) 1990–94, chairman 1994–2000.

**Helge Jung** (1886–1978): Supreme Commander 1944–51.

**Olle Karleby** (1918–94): State Secretary, Ministry of Defence (Social Democratic Party) 1953–59; managing director, Försvarets fabriksverk 1959–63; CEO, Hansa 1966–70; CEO, Trygg-Hansa 1971–73, chairman 1973–78; chairman, Stockholms Köpmansklubb 1971–80.

**Eric Krönmark** (1931–2024): Minister of Defence (Moderate Party) 1976–78 and 1979–81; Governor of Kalmar County 1981–96.

**Bertil Kugelberg** (1900–91): deputy director, Swedish Employers' Confederation (SAF) 1942–46, director 1946–66; board member of Norgehjälpen 1942–45; board member of Europahjälpen 1946–50; board member of the resistance organization 1962–66.

**Jan Leijonhielm** (1944–): assistant, East Economic Bureau 1965–70; source handler, IB 1970–73; GBU 1973–81; director, East Economic Bureau 1981–89; programme director for Russia Studies, Swedish National Defence Research Institute (FOA)

1989–2009; programme director for Intelligence Analysis, Centre for Asymmetric Threats and Terrorist Studies (CATS) 2008–14.

**Alvar Lindencrona** (1910–81): Bachelor of Laws; expert, Ministry of Defence 1940–43; first secretary, Ministry of Communication 1944–45; bureau head, Swedish Aviation Authority 1945–46; CEO, Thule 1947–64; board member of SAAB 1948–80; SAAB Great Britain 1974–79; SAAB-Scania of America 1974–80; chairman, Nationalföreningen för trafiksäkerhetens främjande (NTF) 1949–51; investigator of the Swedish military's regional and local site assets 1953; board member of Skandia 1964–78 (acting 1964–69); chairman, ICC Sweden 1964–81; deputy chairman, ICC International Court of Arbitration 1977–81; commander of the resistance organization 1949–78; father of Elisabeth and Gustaf, Jr.

**Elisabeth Lindencrona Paues** (1942–): language teacher at the EU Commission 1992–2005; daughter of Alvar.

**Gustaf Lindencrona, Jr.** (1938–): Professor Emeritus in Financial Law; Chancellor, Stockholm University 1994–2003; son of Alvar.

**Gustaf Lindencrona, Sr.** (1871–1952): bureau director, Board for Public Roads and Water Structures 1910–37; father of Alvar.

**Stig Malm** (1942–2021): chairman, Swedish Trade Union Confederation (LO) 1983–91.

**Eije Mossberg** (1908–97): State Secretary, Ministry of Social Affairs (Social Democratic Party) 1944–45, Deputy Minister 1945–47; Minister of the Interior 1947–51; Governor of Kopparberg County 1951–57; board member of the resistance organization 1949–51.

**Gunnar Nilsson** (1922–97): deputy chairman, Swedish Trade Union Confederation (LO) 1971–73, chairman 1973–83.

**Torsten Nilsson** (1905–97): Minister of Defence (Social Democratic Party) 1951–57; Minister of Foreign Affairs 1962–71.

**Torsten Nothin** (1884–1972): Minister of Justice (Social Democratic Party) 1924–26; Governor of Stockholm 1933–49; chairman, Nationalföreningen för trafiksäkerhetens främjande (NTF) 1934–38; chairman, the Defence Commission 1949–53.

**Svante Nycander** (1933–2024): Licentiate Political Science; author; trade union correspondent, *Dagens Nyheter* 1969–74, leader writer 1974–79, chief political editor 1979–94.

**Thede Palm** (1907–95): PhD History of Religion; author; deputy librarian, Lund University Library 1938–56 (on leave from 1943); employee, C Bureau 1940–46; chief, T Bureau 1946–64; director of research, Swedish Military Academy 1965–72; staff writer, *Svenska Dagbladet* 1965–95; deputy editor, *Svensk Tidskrift* 1967–79; operations director of the resistance organization 1949–66.

**Olof Palme** (1927–86): political advisor, Prime Minister's Office (Social Democratic Party) 1954–61, bureau head 1961–65; Minister of Communication 1965–67; Prime Minister 1969–76 and 1982–86.

**Carl Persson** (1919–2014): State Secretary, Ministry of the Interior (Social Democratic Party) 1958–64; National Police Commissioner 1964–78.

**Thage G. Peterson** (1933–): Minister of Defence (Social Democratic Party) 1994–97.

**Ingrid Rosander** (1936–): executive secretary; daughter of Astrid Tunell; childhood friend of the family of Alvar Lindencrona.

**Per Rudberg** (1922–2010): Chief of the Navy 1978–84.

**Michael Sahlin** (1945–): PhD Political Science; secretary, the Submarine Defence Commission 1982–83; chief secretary, the Defence Committee 1984; administrative director, Parliamentary Defence Committee 1987–91; chief secretary, the Defence

Committee 1988; chairman, the government's Defence Commission 1991–92; State Secretary, Ministry of Defence (Moderate Party) 1991–94; ambassador to Turkey 1995–98, former Yugoslavia 2000–02, Norway 2007–10.

**Per Edvin Sköld** (1891–1972): Minister of Defence (Social Democratic Party) 1938–45; Minister of Finance 1949–55.

**Håkan Sterky** (1900–92): Doctor of Technology; Professor of Telephony and Telegraphy, Royal Institute of Technology (KTH) 1939–42; executive director, Swedish Telecommunications Authority 1942–65; chairman, Swedish National Defence Research Institute (FOA) 1945–54; board member of the Atomic Committee 1945–65; board member of Atombolaget 1947–68; board member of the resistance organization.

**Gunnar Sträng** (1906–92): chairman, Swedish Agricultural Workers' Union 1939–51; Minister of Finance (Social Democratic Party) 1955–76.

**Nils Swedlund** (1898–1965): Chief of the Defence Staff 1947–51; Supreme Commander 1951–61; board member of the resistance organization.

**Björn von Sydow** (1945–): Reader in Political Science; assistant to Tage Erlander 1970–74; Minister of Defence (Social Democratic Party) 1997–2002; Speaker of the Swedish Parliament 2002–06.

**Stig Synnergren** (1915–2004): Supreme Commander 1970–78.

**Georg Thulin** (1902–90): chief, Swedish State Police (and Security Service) 1938–63.

**Astrid Tunell** (1907–99): secretary to Alvar Lindencrona; childhood friend of his sister and his wife's sisters; mother of Ingrid Rosander.

**Göran Tunhammar** (1946–): director, Swedish Employers' Confederation (SAF) 1990–2001; Confederation of Swedish Enterprise 2001–03.

**Östen Undén** (1886–1974): Minister of Foreign Affairs (Social Democratic Party) 1924–26 and 1945–62.

**Allan Vougt** (1895–1953): Minister of Defence (Social Democratic Party) 1945–51.

**Hans Wermdalen** (1936–): bureau chief, Swedish Security Service 1970–75; head of security, Ericsson 1975–85; deputy managing director, Securitas 1985–2003.

# Chronology

1940 Germany invades Norway. Sweden's intelligence service creates an embryonic resistance organization called "Homeland Stewardship".

1947 In Poland, the Communist Party's power is sanctioned by massive electoral fraud.

1948 Prague coup in Czechoslovakia. Barely hours later, Finland is forced to sign a security policy pact with the Soviet Union.

1949 Prime Minister Tage Erlander issues letters authorizing the formation of a civil resistance organization, to be activated in the event of a Soviet occupation of Sweden, whose activities expand on those of "Homeland Stewardship". Insurance company executive Alvar Lindencrona is appointed as its first commander.

1950 The Korean War breaks out, exacerbating the Cold War.

1951 The Swedish resistance organization's relationship to the Western powers is defined and delimited.

1952 A criminal investigation into a private resistance initiative threatens to expose the Swedish resistance organization that has been sanctioned by the Prime Minister.

| | |
|---|---|
| **1955** | The Swedish resistance organization is legalized through a secret governmental decision. |
| **1962** | Cuban Missile Crisis. |
| **1968** | The Soviet Union crushes the Prague Spring in Czechoslovakia. |
| **1973** | The "IB Affair" exposes the existence of Sweden's secret intelligence service. |
| **1978** | Curt-Steffan Giesecke, director of the Swedish Employers' Confederation, takes over Alvar Lindencrona's covert duties. Emergence of the resistance organization's second generation of members. |
| **1979** | The Soviet Union invades Afghanistan. |
| **1981** | Soviet submarine *U-137* runs aground in the Gåsefjärden archipelago inside a Swedish military security zone. |
| **1984** | Submarine hunting initiated in the Karlskrona archipelago. Swedish defence forces open fire on foreign underwater vessels and military divers. |
| **1989** | Fall of the Berlin Wall. |
| **1991** | Boris Yeltsin declares the dissolution of the Soviet Union. In Sweden, the resistance organization continues its activities despite having been exposed in the media. |
| **1992** | The government's decision on defence spending withdraws state funding for the resistance organization. |
| **1994–95** | Robert Lugn, a former head of the National Home Guard, succeeds Curt-Steffan Giesecke. Emergence of the resistance organization's third generation of members. |

# Prologue

## SUNDAY WALKS

"My father never revealed a secret. If you told him something in confidence, you could rely on him not to breathe a word of it to anyone else," recalls Bengt, now in his fifties. "You knew you could trust him."*[1] There was another side to the coin, however, at least from Bengt's perspective: his father Torsten also kept quiet about his own secrets. One summer the family was passing through the Swedish city of Örebro en route to the west coast. Bengt, who had a fascination with abandoned and off-limits city spaces, asked his father if "the Zone" – Sweden's national wartime headquarters – was nearby. When Torsten answered no, explaining that he had been there, Bengt asked if he could tell him where "the Zone" was in fact located. Bengt remembers his father's frustrating response: "He looked at me, shook his head, and replied with a smile, 'No, I can't do that.'"

Secretiveness may not always be a virtue in families but elsewhere it can be a necessity. Such is the case with the armed forces in which Torsten spent his entire working life, first as an officer and later as a reserve officer trade union representative – or with an underground resistance movement. The latter is not a fanciful invention. Several years after Torsten's death,

*Surnames withheld by request of the family.

Bengt's mother Ulrika told him that his father had been part of a secret civilian group that would be activated in the event of a Russian occupation of Sweden. After retiring from union work in the mid-1990s, Torsten regularly attended meetings with this group in an apartment in central Stockholm. Curiously, its members also included Curt-Steffan Giesecke, a former director of what is now the Confederation of Swedish Enterprise (at that time SAF). On each occasion Torsten received a payment, with which he took Ulrika to dinner, as she put it, "at a fancy restaurant".

When Bengt first learned of his father's hidden life, a great many things suddenly seemed to make sense. At Torsten's funeral, the mourners had included a number of elderly men whom the family did not recognize. Each had placed flowers on the casket and offered their condolences, yet none was willing to explain how he came to know Torsten. Indeed, they exerted themselves to avoid the question. "Ordinary people say things like 'we worked together,'" Bengt recalls, "but these old chaps were too slippery to be pinned down." For a long time after, he had wondered at the odd behaviour of the unknown mourners. Was this the answer?

Bengt also remembered curious incidents from his childhood that he could now connect to what his mother had revealed. Once, during a friendly boxing match with his son, Torsten had let slip: "You should know that I've been trained in hand-to-hand combat by the Norwegians who launched the sabotage raid on the Telemark heavy water factory." The disclosure caught Bengt by surprise: it was out of character for his father to speak openly about such matters. And why would an officer in the Swedish Air Defence Regiment, a unit responsible for missile defence against aerial threats, have been trained in hand-to-hand combat – and by someone from the famed Linge unit of the Norwegian resistance movement? Torsten, it was true, had kept a service weapon "hidden somewhere" at home until he retired, but his reference to training in hand-to-hand combat sounded like something far more advanced.

We now know that Torsten, while doing his officer training at the Military Academy at Karlberg, had become acquainted with Allan Mann. Famous as a close-combat instructor in the Swedish Armed Forces, Mann had allegedly been one of only three Swedes in the Linge unit (though he did not take part in the heavy water sabotage operation in 1943).[2] Was this the connection that Torsten had been referring to? Or was it something else entirely?

On Sundays in the late 1970s and early 1980s, Torsten often took Bengt and his older brother and their mother for walks in the woods north of Stockholm. These walks always ended at military locations. "This is a mobilization depot," Torsten would explain to the family. "What were we doing there?" muses Bengt: "It was as if he was checking on something." And what exactly was Torsten's union work, which allowed him to travel all over Sweden and form a wide network of contacts in Finland, Denmark and Norway, the latter both NATO countries?

"Perhaps it really was just union work," Bengt reflects. As he points out, when a parent is involved in something mysterious in one part of their life, the child must always keep two possibilities in mind – "the thrilling and the realistic" – rather than seeking the more appealing explanation.

Regardless of what applies in this particular case, Bengt thinks it highly likely that his father was a member of a resistance movement: "He cared passionately about Sweden, the Swedish people, and our way of life – our freedom to express ourselves and live the way we want." Bengt relates how he and Torsten were attending a military parade on Army Day in central Stockholm when, as one contemporary newspaper account described it, "helicopters swooped in low over the roofs and lowered soldiers to the ground" and peace activists held up banners with slogans about disarmament.[3] Bengt had wondered if Torsten felt angry. "No," his father had replied. "My job is to defend them and their right to say such things."

Torsten had no doubts about where the greatest threat to Swedish freedoms and democracy lay. When the Soviet Union collapsed, an exhilarated Bengt asked his father whether he, too, saw it as a wonderful development. His father's reply was immediate and ran sharply contrary to the talk of "the end of history" then in vogue in Sweden and much of the West at that time: "You can never trust the Russians."

---

The idea that Torsten was part of a resistance movement would be easy to dismiss as a family legend were it not for the fact that much of Bengt's testimony is echoed by numerous families in Sweden and neighbouring countries quite independently of each other. Families such as Wilhelm's, for example. Wilhelm, an army reserve officer in the Swedish city of Borås, owned a ready-to-wear garment factory that manufactured uniforms and protective clothing. His son Curt, now a retired doctor in his seventies, relates how Wilhelm told him and his brother, some time after the end of the Cold War when both boys were adults, that he had "been part of a secret organization".*[4] In the event of an occupation, his task in the organization would have been to exfiltrate individuals in Borås who needed special protection, such as business leaders and local politicians, and hide them in the surrounding countryside.

Like Bengt's childhood memories from a later period, Curt remembers how his father Wilhelm in the 1950s and 1960s regularly took him on Sunday walks to the Tränningen Nature Reserve and the area of Västergötland County formerly known as Norska Skogsbygden, which contained mobilization depots with weapons and other military equipment. Their excursions often led to Bosjön, a lake south of Borås, where it felt to Curt as though his father "wanted to check on things and monitor a particular area to see if it had changed". He speculates that his father was reconnoitring the terrain as preparation for a future evacuation of key individuals. His younger brother Olof, who

*Surname withheld by request of the family.

partly followed their father in becoming a reserve officer, has a similar recollection: "We often found ourselves in isolated locations, quite unlike a destination chosen for a regular stroll."[5]

In recent years, there has been an open discussion in Denmark about the existence of Cold War-era civilian intelligence and resistance networks that were approved by key figures in Danish military intelligence, such as Hans Lunding, its influential director during the 1950s.[6] Otto Grøn, father of marine archaeologist Ole Grøn, worked as a dentist while holding a top position in one of these networks.[7] Now in his sixties, Ole Grøn can relate to stories told by Bengt and the brothers Curt and Olof about Sunday walks with the family that seemed normal at the time but that perhaps had a secondary purpose. He recalls that he was similarly used as a cover by his father when arranging to meet individuals connected to the resistance movement.[8] For example, Copenhagen airport was a key hub for the network, and in those days Otto's father would often take his son on a boys-only excursion for the ostensible purpose of watching aircraft.

Other circumstances lend weight to these men's belief that their fathers were not merely part of a covert group committed to waging an armed campaign against occupying forces but members of an organization, created by Sweden's Prime Minister at the start of the Cold War for the specific purpose of leading civilian resistance on Swedish soil, that for many years effectively formed part of Swedish defence planning. There can be no doubt that such an organization existed. While researching this book I have met with the adult children of known members, all of whom have had similar experiences. Intelligence officers, senior politicians with special knowledge, and former resistance personnel have explained to me the organization's methods. Not least, I have examined previously unknown or classified documents that provide insights into its workings. The reason why Bengt, Curt and Olof could put two and two together and connect their families' experiences to this organization was because its covert activities had finally seen the light of day.

## THE POPULAR IMAGE OF THE RESISTANCE MOVEMENT

In the early 1990s, the Swedish parliament appointed a neutrality commission whose directives included ascertaining Sweden's military and political contacts with the West during the Cold War, specifically the period 1949–69. One of those deposed was Ingemar Engman, a former public official and intelligence officer. Engman testified that a civil resistance organization dedicated to waging armed struggle against occupying Russian forces had "managed to remain largely secret during all these years".[9] "But," he added, "there was a passage in that book by Calle Persson..."

In 1990, former National Police Commissioner Carl "Calle" Persson had mentioned in his memoirs that he had been part of a "group responsible for contingency planning in the event of a foreign occupation".[10] The remark, Engman explained, had whetted the public's curiosity. In December that year, *Dagens Nyheter*, Sweden's leading daily, published a front-page article confirming the organization's existence. Its author, a journalist named Bjarne Stenquist, gave a thrilling account of how in 1958, the year Carl Persson claimed to have joined it, Sweden had established a "resistance organization" that was subsequently led by Alvar Lindencrona, an insurance company director, for 20 years "without the knowledge of either parliament or the electorate". A clear violation of Sweden's official status as a non-aligned, neutral country, this covert organization had worked closely with Western intelligence services and, above all, the CIA.[11]

Only a handful of senior public figures, including Prime Minister Tage Erlander, Interior Minister Rune Johansson, Swedish Trade Union Confederation (LO) leader Arne Geijer, and Swedish Employers' Confederation leader Bertil Kugelberg, knew of its existence. Together, they monitored the activities of what *Dagens Nyheter* described as a "Swedish guerrilla force", which was organized into regional leaderships and provided with weapons and insurgency training tactics. According to Stenquist, the organization's responsibilities also included establishing radio contact with the West and facilitating the evacuation of the royal family and the political leadership to headquarters in exile in the United Kingdom, a NATO country. The initiative behind the organization's founding had been taken in the early 1950s by William Colby, a CIA officer at the United States embassy in Stockholm. It was Colby's own "'stay-behind' organization", as Stenquist put it, that had been transferred to the Swedish state. Yet the American connection had been maintained. *Dagens Nyheter* claimed that Sweden's resistance organization had gradually been integrated into a network of similar agencies that the CIA "established" across Western Europe. The existence of other groups also came to light in the early 1990s, when archives suddenly opened up following the collapse of the Berlin Wall and there was broad public interest in coming to terms with the past.

In summer 1992, Christer Larsson, a journalist for Swedish Radio, pursued the subject in a series of reports that described other areas of military cooperation between Sweden and NATO during the Cold War. These revelations had the immediate consequence of prompting the conservative coalition government under Prime Minister Carl Bildt to appoint a neutrality commission (albeit limiting its scope to the period before 1969, just prior to Olof Palme's politically controversial first term of office as Prime Minister).[12] In the 1950s, Larsson claimed, the United States and the United Kingdom had sent personnel such as William Colby to Sweden in order to establish "resistance networks that initially operated entirely beyond Sweden's control".[13] He also cited documents which allegedly confirmed that Sweden's resistance organization, having eventually been brought under Swedish command in the late 1950s, "was incorporated into NATO's programme for other military resistance organizations".

By the time Larsson's reports aired on the radio, there had already been further revelations about an organization whose existence had long been a well-kept secret – indeed, one of the "most secret of all secrets".[14] In August 1991, *Dagens Nyheter* published another article by Stenquist in which he revealed that the resistance organization remained active and that it had a new leader, Curt-Steffan Giesecke.[15] (Giesecke flatly denied the claim.) The article also shed light for the first time on the role played in the organization by the representatives for labour and employers. According to Stenquist, the Trade Union Confederation (Landsorganisationen, LO), the Employers' Confederation (Svenska Arbetsgivareföreningen, SAF), the Confederation of Professional Employees (Tjänstemännens centralorganisation, TCO) and the Federation of Swedish Farmers (Lantbrukarnas Riksförbund, LRF) were all included in a governing committee intended to give the organization a "foundation that crossed party boundaries and social groups". The committee may also have been intended to function as a new national ruling body in the event of the Swedish government and royal family being captured or killed. "This organization has never been 'legal' in the strictly legal sense," claimed Stenquist's anonymous source in *Dagens Nyheter*. "It was for this reason that anchoring it in a broad range of interest groups was so vital. Under no circumstances could the new national leadership seem to represent the interests of a particular stratum of society."

Four years later, in 1996, two members of the resistance organization appeared in public for the first time by allowing themselves to be interviewed for a television documentary produced by journalist Thomas Kanger.[16] The members in question were Carl Eric Almgren, a former head of the army, and a hotelier named Reinhold Geijer. Almgren, who claimed to have served in the resistance organization's leadership in the 1960s and 1970s, revealed that between four and five hundred Swedes had been involved. He also confirmed that Curt-Steffan Giesecke had been the organization's national director.

Geijer related that he himself had been the regional director in the northern Swedish counties of Jämtland, Härjedalen and Västerbotten, and later also Västernorrland, as well as being in charge of a number of smaller cells, comprising around 70 men in total. Prior to the publication of this book, he was the only person at this level of command to have voluntarily admitted to being part of the resistance organization.

Kanger and another journalist, Oscar Hedin, re-interviewed Geijer in 1998 for a feature article in *Dagens Nyheter* about the resistance organization's regional structure. In it, Geijer claimed to have received training in Britain that included "dead letter drops for handing over secret messages and other James Bond-like exercises".[17] With the help of surviving documents, the two journalists were also able to show that a travelling businessman had for a period been the organization's regional director in the counties of Småland and Östergötland; we will return to him later on.

Several years were to pass before the resistance organization again found itself in the public eye. In *The Secret Alliance*, a highly publicized book which appeared in Swedish in 2011, defence journalist Mikael Holmström described in detail how Sweden, from the formation of NATO right to the end of the Cold War, secretly cooperated with Western powers and made preparations for receiving help in the event of a Soviet invasion. At the time, it was the fullest account of what later researchers have called the "*mutual dependence* between NATO and Sweden". That dependence, as Tuomas Forsberg and Magnus Christiansson have argued in their recent work, derived from Sweden's "need for coordination and help in a war situation" and NATO's "need for a strong Swedish defence and early warning" on its northern flank against a potential Soviet offensive, a relationship that challenges the hoary cliché of Cold War-era Sweden as merely a "mediator, critic and bridge" between the superpowers.[18]

Holmström devoted a whole section to the resistance organization, providing new information that significantly extended the public's understanding of its activities.[19] His analysis relied on the diaries of former premier Tage Erlander and other documents that had not been freely available in the 1990s. He was also able to draw on the first published study of the resistance organization, which showed that the organization dated as far back as 1949, thereby contradicting Stenquist's claim in *Dagens Nyheter* that it had evolved from an established Western-led network.[20]

Holmström accepted this finding. However, he argued that it had also cooperated extensively with the Western powers, as the organizations's own name made clear: "Swedes in the know called the resistance organization *Stay behind.* The choice of an English phrase was deliberate. This was an international trend involving similar organizations in a range of NATO countries."[21] Although Thomas Kanger had also used the term "Stay behind" in his TV documentary as a name for Sweden's resistance movement in the mid-1990s, it was thanks to Holmström's book that it entered general circulation. Holmström also publicly identified several other "Swedes in the know", among them Håkan Sterky, head of the Swedish Telecommunications Authority, and Thede Palm, a historian of religion who served as chief of the intelligence agency known as T Bureau between the end of World War II and the mid-1960s.

In interviews with Holmström, who has graciously shared his research notes with me, Curt-Steffan Giesecke, former director of the Employers' Confederation, publicly admitted that he had indeed been in charge of the resistance organization right up to and beyond the collapse of the Soviet Union. According to Holmström, its activities continued under new leadership until the organization was mothballed after the turn of the millennium.

---

This, in broad strokes, is what has hitherto been generally known about the resistance organization. Obviously, there is more to be discovered and numerous claims to be substantiated or refuted, certainly with regard to the organization's activities during and directly after the Cold War, a period that now has little to do with Sweden's national security interest and, with it, any legitimate demand for secrecy. It is also clear that the task of writing the organization's history has been left to journalists, albeit highly able ones. Although a handful of official inquiries, including the Neutrality Policy Commission mentioned earlier, have touched on the resistance organization, their public reports have presented little beyond what was already circulating in the media. In many cases, the most important information remained classified and was carefully filed away in investigators' archives. One of these inquiries, the Security Policy Inquiry led by ambassador Rolf Ekeus, even seems to have been guilty of misleading the public by claiming that "the *Stay behind* issue had a negligible significance, if any, for Sweden's security policy between 1969 and 1989".[22]

Almost the only scholar to have carried out significant primary research on this unique episode in modern Swedish history is Magnus Hjort, who has authored two studies of the personal papers of key Swedish policymakers, which I have developed in consultation with Hjort.[23] Other scholarship on the resistance organization, by contrast, has been largely based on secondary sources.[24] My investigation, which relies on not only oral interviews with identified subjects but also – and, methodologically, more importantly – hitherto unexamined written sources, deepens our understanding of the resistance movement. Indeed, in this regard, it must be considered a pioneering study. It is, of course, impossible to present a fully comprehensive, coherent or systematic account of activities that were always meant to remain covert and thus resist full documentation. Nonetheless, my study ranges far beyond our existing knowledge of the resistance organization and complicates the information about it that has already been made available.

Research on social and political history almost never claims to be the final word. It is, rather, an iterative process that involves ongoing revisions and corrections in an attempt to get closer to the truth, as previously unknown or overlooked sources continue to shed new light on incidents and phenomena relating to the topic in question. My hope is therefore that this "first draft" will inspire more individuals with personal knowledge of these historic events to come forward with more pieces of the puzzle. Lastly, my approach differs from earlier accounts of this subject in how I interpret Sweden's covert resistance organization and my reasons for wanting to tell its story.*

## A NECESSARY REASSESSMENT

Until now, studies of the resistance organization have been premised on the assumption that it was somehow morally suspect or undemocratic in nature. Thomas Kanger's television documentary from the 1990s began by ambushing members of the Parliamentary Defence Committee and forcing them to admit on camera that they had no idea what the term "Stay behind" meant. Kanger then made dramatic claims that decisions about the resistance organization had been made "without any democratic oversight" and that "responsibility for the nation's survival had been given to a social elite rather than elected representatives".

A similar but more restrained critique was also implicit in the first articles on the resistance movement that appeared in

*There is a widespread view that scholars should not have personal opinions about their subject. Research on social and political history should be "objective" and "stick to the facts", we are told. In practice, this is an untenable position, as Gunnar Myrdal, winner of the Nobel Prize in Economics, observes in his book *Objectivity in Social Research*. All social and political research is coloured by the researcher's own views. The choice of subject itself reflects moral and political valuations, as does the way the researcher chooses to organize facts and analysis. The question is thus: how should the researcher deal with this problem – by being open about such valuations, or by hiding them? Myrdal's view, with which I concur, is that honesty and transparency on this issue are the only way to carry out legitimate social and political research that lends itself to scrutiny and critique. This does not, of course, mean that the results themselves should be inflected by the researcher's opinions.

the pages of *Dagens Nyheter*. Holmström may have been largely correct with regard to the factual information he presented, but, at least as I see it, his analysis was skewed by his conviction that the formation of the resistance organization was closely bound up with Sweden's military collaboration with NATO during the Cold War, something he believed the Swedish electorate should have been informed about.

Other accounts have taken an even more critical approach, as illustrated by Swiss author Daniele Ganser in the chapter on Sweden, which he co-wrote with Mats Deland, in his speculative and error-filled book *NATO's Secret Armies*.[25] Ganser and Deland claim that the Swedish resistance organization was one of several subversive, extreme-right armed groups in Western Europe which operated under American and British control during the Cold War, and that its origins can be traced back to the Swedish Nazi organization Sveaborg.[26]

Such claims that the resistance organization was an undemocratic project or an extension of NATO have always seemed far-fetched to me. My own instinctive view is that, on the contrary, Sweden's resistance organization was an admirable and well-intentioned initiative whose activities badly need to be demythologized. That conviction has only been strengthened by the empirical data which I present in this study. Sweden's resistance organization was truly Swedish – indeed, it was the continuation of a policy that Sweden had already adopted during World War II – and not some foreign import. It was not, as a new Swedish glossary of Cold War terminology claims, "inspired by the West".[27] Quite the opposite: the Western powers were deliberately and explicitly kept at arm's length, perhaps even excessively so.

The resistance movement was also firmly anchored in Sweden's constitution and democracy, partly by virtue of a hitherto unknown government decision and partly because the resistance organization can be seen as an offshoot of Sweden's corporative model of governance. Admittedly, the organization was highly classified, but this was for justifiable reasons relating to the need to protect sensitive activities, not to hide double-dealing with NATO by Swedish politicians and civil servants. As I see it, the resistance organization's members were patriots who wanted to protect Sweden against the very real threat of occupation. As hotelier Reinhold Geijer explained in a television interview: "All of us were utterly committed to the task and felt that we were doing a service for our country."[28]

The limited research on the often mythologized resistance organizations that were set up in other Western countries – Norway, Denmark, the Netherlands, West Germany, Switzerland, Italy and France – has reached similar conclusions. Resistance organizations were established as a national mission to counter, at the local level, the global threat posed by Soviet communism. In many cases, they represented the continuation of resistance movements that had resisted occupying German forces during World War II. Admittedly, Britain and the United States, both powerful NATO members, played a far greater role in financing and coordinating these other organizations than they did Sweden's. However, there is nothing to support the widespread perception that Cold War resistance organizations were the sinister puppets of foreign powers. On the contrary, "a common thread seems to be a jealous effort, almost everywhere, to retain a close national control of the institution".[29]

Even in the most famous instance, Italy's *Gladio* network, which has been accused of carrying out domestic terrorist acts in order to stir up political opposition against the Italian Left in the 1960s and 1970s, such conspiratorial claims have proven groundless. *Gladio* was established in order to counter an invasion of Italian territory by Soviet forces as part of a larger assault on Western Europe through Yugoslavia and Italy. But even though the CIA enjoyed exceptionally close ties to the Italian resistance organization, these were not so strong as to prevent Italy's leaders from rejecting American requests to be allowed to use *Gladio* "for the function of propaganda, counter-propaganda and disturbance".[30]

Revising this history is, I believe, of crucial importance for Sweden's – and Europe's – self-perception. At present, there is a broad consensus that Sweden showed a lack of courage during a crucial juncture in world history. It is often argued that Sweden's foreign and security policies accommodated Nazi Germany during World War II and the Soviet Union during the Cold War. And yet, as scholars such as military historian Kent Zetterberg have shown, Sweden's support for other Nordic countries and the Allies shaped its policies during World War II to a far greater extent than the handful of relatively limited concessions it made to Germany during the desperate early years of the war when Sweden faced its greatest peril and needed breathing space in which to build up its military. As Zetterberg remarks pithily, "Sweden was anything but a German satellite or a country of eugenicists, Nazis, and political collaborators."[31]

My research on the Swedish resistance organization during the Cold War likewise shows that Sweden's stance towards the Soviet Union is more complex than the prevailing narrative suggests. The key actors – the Swedish government, trade unions, agricultural bodies and private enterprise – all saw Soviet communism for what it was and formed a united front in covertly planning how to protect Sweden against it. Many Swedes also made vital individual contributions, in many cases at considerable costs to their family and professional lives, in order to make these plans for civil resistance in Sweden into a practical reality. All of these people deserve our grateful recognition.

Promoting a more positive understanding of Sweden's recent past is especially important during these politically turbulent times. National pride is vital to a people's willingness to defend their country, as Ukraine's soldiers and civilians have impressively demonstrated in the wake of the Russian invasion of February 2022. For the same reason, it is imperative that Europe and the Western world in general resist the prevailing tendency to interpret post-war history in conspiratorial, anti-American and anti-nationalist terms, and instead seek a more nuanced understanding of these events and actors.

I also believe that the history of the Cold War resistance organization contains important lessons for Sweden and the West. As a recuperative project, it shows how comparable or similar structures could be created and how they might operate within the framework of comprehensive defence planning, something that has once again become a bulwark of national survival. This study's documenting of the thoroughly national origins of the Swedish resistance organization is equally important in light of Sweden's changed national security policy, its accession as a NATO member in March 2024, and the stresses placed upon the military alliance in recent years. Those origins have the potential to form the framework for a "patriotic" NATO – a notion to which I will return in my conclusion.

Sweden and the West also have much to learn from the resistance organization more broadly. When the COVID-19 pandemic broke out in spring 2020, it quickly became apparent that many countries were woefully unprepared. As became clear in Sweden, materiel that could have been of practical use in a worst-case scenario had been needlessly destroyed. At the end of the Cold War, Sweden had 35 mobile hospitals each with a 200-bed capacity as well as 15 smaller naval field hospitals on its coasts, almost all of which were subsequently decommissioned as part of the broader process of détente and disarmament in the 1990s. In the early 2000s, Sweden's last field hospitals were donated to other countries and more than 600 unused respirators were discarded.[32]

To take a comparable instance from the United Kingdom, a British parliamentary enquiry into the COVID-19 emergency concluded that the Department of Health and Social Care "had no plan before the pandemic for how it might increase critical care equipment in the event of an emergency".[33] Just one example of the serious deficiencies in resistance capacity – alas, there are many others – it highlights the need for clear-headedness in national security planning, including for scenarios outside the current parameters. Western states, in addition to creating new structures for civilian resistance in the event of war or a threat to national security, need to establish in their governance structures the fundamental sense of responsibility and agency that Sweden's secret resistance organization – and its counterparts – showed during the Cold War.

---

In the following chapters, I present the empirical core of this study, which comprises seven chapters arranged into three sections. In each case, the historical focus is on the early decades of the Cold War, partly because of the nature of the archival material but also partly in response to the confusion that exists today over the origins and structure of the Swedish resistance organization. In Part I, I move from the broader context of the Cold War to concentrate on the threat scenario during the years immediately following 1945 in order to determine how far Sweden's civilian resistance organization was based on rational considerations of *realpolitik*. In Part II, I address the question of the resistance's leadership by providing biographical sketches of leading figures within what I call the organization's first generation. The third and final empirical section describes, from the perspectives of those at the bottom as well as the top, how the resistance organization was created and developed as well as how it began to be dismantled during the second generation.

The Epilogue opens by summarizing my most important findings, after which I discuss in greater detail the ways in which present-day Sweden and the West more broadly can learn from the resistance organization. In the book's Afterwords, I first provide an extended discussion of my sources and research methodology. Finally, I conclude the study by returning to the level of the individual and examining the human costs of the idealistic activities of the Swedish resistance organization.

# PART ONE

# Invasion

# 1

# A Possible Scenario

## ATTACK ON SWEDEN

War came to Sweden on a warm day in September 1992, the time of year when weather conditions in the Baltic Sea are ideal for an invasion. For Soviet military leadership, the occupation of Sweden had become a logical necessity. Its top-ranking officers feared that the Western powers would intervene on behalf of democratic protest movements in the USSR's increasingly unstable Baltic and Eastern European satellite republics. Taking control of Sweden would seal off the Baltic region from the West, giving the USSR free rein to brutally suppress the popular uprisings in progress. There were also other significant advantages to seizing Sweden's territory in a sudden attack. Sudden proximity to the new Soviet border would bring Denmark and Norway into line, and conditions for controlling the strategically important North Atlantic in a confrontation with American forces in the near or distant future would be greatly improved.

The Soviet Union's General Secretary, once famous as a reformer but now in thrall to militant circles in Moscow seeking to "restore law and order" to the empire, had reluctantly accepted the plan's military and territorial advantages. Largely as a matter of form, he now gave his approval to an attack on

Sweden, whose codename referred to a world-famous Swedish film actress.

Despite the favourable sea conditions, the attack did not begin with the Soviet Navy blocking the horizon with a fearsome assembly of minesweepers, corvettes, frigates, destroyers, cruisers, military landing craft and civilian car ferries. A D-Day-style invasion stood little chance of success if Sweden was given time to raise its guard. As its armada headed towards Sweden's territorial waters, the Soviet Union therefore needed to delay Swedish efforts to mobilize. By means of radio signals to Sweden, it activated a network of "illegals" or sleeper agents, who for years had been standing ready to carry out acts of sabotage and liquidation with the support of arriving *spetsnaz* units. These agents now went to work.

On 3 September, the day before the invasion, the energy supply to Stockholm and other parts of Sweden had been mysteriously disrupted. Large numbers of fighter jets developed mechanical problems, and many of the air force's pilots were attacked on air bases and at home by Swedish-speaking assailants posing as drivers, contractors and door-to-door evangelists. On the following day, the sky was filled with hundreds of Soviet fighter jets and bombers whose primary mission was to disable Sweden's air defences and destroy its military runways. These were followed by transport aircraft that dropped paratroopers whose mission was to seize control of the commercial airports of Sweden's major cities. In Stockholm, a Soviet attack helicopter swooped down on Ragnar Östberg's iconic City Hall and opened fire with a minigun.

Once the invading forces had established bridgeheads, Soviet ships began to rapidly unload more troops and heavy materiel using the large ferry terminal at Trelleborg in the south and the island ports of Gotland. In less than a week, Soviet ground forces in Sweden outnumbered the defenders by a factor of two or three. If external help did not arrive soon, the battle for Sweden's survival as an independent nation would seem to be over.

The preceding narrative is a rough summary of a much-talked-about novel titled *Operation Garbo* that was issued in May 1988 by Timbro, a publishing house sponsored by Swedish business interests.[1] Its pseudonymous author "Harry Winter" was in fact three leading figures in an ongoing debate about Swedish military preparedness: Lars Christiansson, a defence reporter; Ingemar Dörfer, research director of the Swedish National Defence Institute (FOA); and Bo Hugemark, an army colonel. In presenting a fictional account of a Soviet attack on Sweden in the near future, the trio hoped to make the general public aware of what they regarded as a very real threat scenario.[2]

For the authors, who did not have the benefit of our hindsight, it was simply not plausible that the dissolution of the Soviet Union, which the policies of Mikhail Gorbachev and much else at the time suggested was imminent, would be a peaceful process. Hawkish forces could easily seize power and decide that, in order to prevent the collapse of the Soviet Union, they needed to initiate a large-scale military operation that Sweden would be drawn into. They were not alone in this view, as is evident from the fact that, on 6 November 1989, just three days before the fall of the Berlin Wall, Swedish authorities began an exercise in "heightened psychological preparedness" by sending an official pamphlet titled *If War Comes* to every national media outlet.[3] Preparations were also being made to mass distribute the pamphlet at short notice.

The dramatic winter of 1989/90 even saw an incident that echoed some of the events depicted in *Operation Garbo*. Swedish intelligence became aware that the Politburo had "taken a decision to intervene militarily in the Baltics but that Gorbachev had secured a temporary respite in which to try to convince the Baltic nations by political means [to remain in the Soviet Union]".[4] By the time observers judged Gorbachev's diplomatic initiative to have failed, the USSR's now weakened military forces had already been deployed in an attempt to halt resurgent independence movements in the Caucasus. Soviet interference in the Baltics was limited to the failed coup attempts that took place in the Lithuanian and Latvian capitals in January 1991. Before the end of the year, Boris Yeltsin had acknowledged the dissolution of the Soviet Union and recognized the independence of its former satellite republics. The basis for the political assumptions made by *Operation Garbo*'s authors no longer existed.

*Operation Garbo*'s value today lies in its depiction of how Sweden might be invaded, what ambassador Michael Sahlin calls "an ingenious fictional portrayal of a scenario that experts actually thought possible".[5] Sahlin is deservedly regarded as "the embodiment of Swedish defence planning".[6] During the final decade of the Cold War and into the early 1990s, he held several key defence and security policy roles: secretary of the 1983 Submarine Defence Commission; administrative director of the Parliamentary Defence Committee, with secret responsibility for evacuation of the wartime delegation to an underground bunker in Stockholm or the wartime headquarters known as "the Zone"; and State Secretary in the Ministry of Defence.

"The best way to bring a country to its knees, then and now, is to start by cutting off the electricity and taking out essential functions using murder and *spetsnaz* forces. Then you launch pre-emptive bombing strikes and an invasion. There is a kind of logic to it all," explains Sahlin. "Now, given Sweden's location, any attempt to invade us rather than Finland will have to have a naval component. After an initial phase of confusion and degradation, they will have to land in large numbers, and airborne troops will not be enough."

A surprise invasion of this kind was precisely what the Swedish military had come to expect during the latter stages of the Cold War after the Soviet Union's treacherous attacks on Czechoslovakia and Afghanistan.[7] Soviet suppression of the "Prague Spring" in August 1968 – when the Soviet Union, just like in *Operation Garbo*, feared a Western military intervention – began with

Aeroflot jets without flight plans landing at Prague airport and disembarking *spetsnaz* units.[8] In 1979, the Soviet Union gradually infiltrated Afghanistan with over 40,000 men, many of whom had been given Afghan uniforms and language training; they went into action on Christmas Day, when NATO's headquarters were closed for the holiday.[9] The scenario long thought most likely by Sweden's military planners was a concentrated large-scale assault on northern Sweden via an occupied or politically subdued Finland together with another on Sweden's Baltic coast. In both cases, Sweden's defenders would have plenty of notice. After Czechoslovakia and Afghanistan, however, that assumption no longer seemed reasonable.[10]

## "WE WERE SAVED BY THE BELL"

"Those of us in the know were worried. Invasion was a continual possibility," remembers Eric Krönmark, who served as Minister of Defence between 1976 and 1981 in two of Thorbjörn Fälldin's centre-right coalition governments.*[11] For Jan Leijonhielm, who had personally recruited informants in the Soviet Union and was at that time working for what he calls "the firm" (Sweden's clandestine intelligence service IB and its successor GBU), it was "beyond any doubt" that the Soviet Union had drawn up plans for an invasion of Sweden, the details of which closely resembled the invasions of Czechoslovakia and Afghanistan.[12] As illustration, he relates that Swedish intelligence had been informed that the Soviets had manufactured copies of the military uniforms of various NATO countries (and presumably also Sweden's); a week or two before an invasion, some hundred Soviet infiltrators would appear on Swedish soil. Seeming to prove the presence of NATO troops in Sweden, their false uniforms would give the Soviets a pretext for an attack. Alternatively, Leijonhielm explains, the infiltrators could be

* Eric Krönmark died on 12 January 2024.

used to "liquidate selected targets, preferably senior government figures, top military officials, and pilots".

During the 1970s and 1980s, Soviet submarine incursions into Swedish territorial waters increased in number and severity. Leijonhielm claims to have "met Russian personnel who conducted submarines exercises near Swedish cities, in some cases so close as to be able to see people on the beach". A key reason for the Soviet submarine activity in this phase of the Cold War seems to have been preparation for undermining Sweden's capacity to mobilize at the start of an invasion. The author of two books on this subject, Commodore Nils-Ove Jansson, whose experience includes serving as operational director of the navy's submarine search-and-kill programme and deputy chief of Sweden's military intelligence and security service (MUST), emphasizes that sightings of foreign submarines and unauthorized incursions by what seemed to be military divers often took place in close geographical proximity to permanent defence installations such as radar stations and naval bases as well as civilian installations connected to electricity supply and telecommunications, including all of Sweden's nuclear power plants.[13]

Jansson also claims that in the 1980s the nature of these incursions began to change, from conventional reconnaissance operations to more general drills for embarking and disembarking *spetsnaz* units. The mission of these special forces was to plant nuclear mines and other small nuclear devices that could be detonated remotely upon the declaration of hostilities. When Soviet submarine *U-137* went aground in the Blekinge archipelago in south-east Sweden in October 1981, supposedly because of a navigation error, its actual mission was to pick up one such sabotage group, which had landed from another Soviet submarine in order to plant nuclear mines inside the nearby naval base at Karlskrona.[14] "This vessel belonged to *spetsnaz* brigade 561, based in Kaliningrad," Jansson explains. "Its skipper has now even been identified by name."[15]

Lars-Erik De Geer, who was among the Swedish National Defence Institute personnel sent to investigate whether *U-137* was carrying nuclear warheads, goes even further and argues that the submarine "was on a mission to install one or more live nuclear devices in the Karlskrona archipelago".[16] The Chief of the Navy, Admiral Per Rudberg, observed merely that "the incursion [by *U-137*] was deliberate".[17] Yet some support for the more striking claims about the submarine's mission is to be found in the final report made by the bipartisan parliamentary Submarine Defence Commission, which was appointed in response to the *U-137* incident and several others the following year, including a high-profile submarine incursion into the Stockholm archipelago. Convened to "authoritatively determine what took place", the Commission concluded that Soviet submarine activities represented "the preparatory phase of a planned military operation" to launch a surprise attack against Sweden that might involve *spetsnaz* units and "measures connected with the use and clearing of mines".[18,19]

Michael Sahlin, who wrote the final report, contends that the increasingly serious submarine incursions which the Commission investigated in the early 1980s were "what we in Sweden were able to discern" of a far larger military and political context, one whose gravity would only become apparent later. Sahlin is here referring to the fact that the Cold War had entered a period in which the nuclear terror balance between the West and the USSR could be called into question. There were several reasons for this development. First, NATO had in 1979 decided to move highly accurate mid-range ballistic missiles to locations in Western Europe within striking distance of Moscow. Second, the United States had adopted a new "maritime strategy" based on launching attacks against Soviet nuclear submarines from the seas around Scandinavia. And third, the Reagan administration had commissioned the Strategic Defense Initiative, which was intended to establish a defensive shield in space that could protect the US from intercontinental ballistic missiles.

Collectively, these factors had served to convince the Soviets not only that an attack by the West would disable its capacity for Mutually Assured Destruction (MAD) but that such an attack was now imminent. The Soviet leadership drew up detailed plans, which remained in force for the rest of the Cold War, to initiate a full-scale war involving both nuclear weapons and conventional forces at the first indication of a first-strike attack by the West.[20] In such a conflict, Sweden would have been a key front-line theatre and could well have been attacked first. As former Minister of Defence Eric Krönmark observes, "If the Soviets had gained control of Swedish territory, their strategic position would have been radically different." Former intelligence officer Jan Leijonhielm agrees: "Sweden would have been in a dire position. In the long term, it is hard to imagine that Sweden would have escaped occupation. The Soviets would have wanted to move the whole scenario westwards of Norway in order to clash with NATO as far from Russia as possible."

Gunnar Nordbeck, who was Krönmark's State Secretary for Defence, echoed this view in a deposition to the Security Policy Inquiry that was only declassified in 2023:

> Even before the passing of the 1982 Defence Act, our attitude towards security policy had begun to change. We could now imagine the USSR launching a pre-emptive attack on Scandinavia. Their goal would be to take possession of Norway's Atlantic seaboard. [...] The reason for such an attack was the escalation of NATO's presence in Norway and the growing importance of the Soviet base in Murmansk [for the USSR's nuclear attack capabilities]. [...] If war broke out, it could well start in Scandinavia.[21]

This perspective finds confirmation in information acquired even earlier from General Jan Sejna, chief of staff for Czechoslovakia's Minister of Defence, whose defection in 1968 was of crucial importance to Western military planners:

> Regarding Sweden, Sejna related that in 1963 Marshal Rodion Malinovsky, the USSR's Minister of Defence, had informed his [Warsaw Pact] colleagues that Sweden's and Austria's neutrality

> would no longer be respected. [...] In the event of a full-scale war, Sweden was to be attacked on the first day and coup attempts made against its major cities and key ports.[22]

Military preparations to attack Sweden were also visible from the air. From the cockpit of his Lansen and Viggen fighters, Lars-Olov Johansson, a reconnaissance pilot and former director of the Swedish Air Force's intelligence college, was able to follow the large-scale Soviet military exercises named *Zapad* (the Russian for "West") in the 1970s and 1980s, which included a mustering of landing craft in the Baltic Sea. "Would these vessels turn left towards targets in central Sweden close to Norrköping and Stockholm, or right towards the Gulf of Finland and then return to Soviet territorial waters? Every time I wondered," he recalls.[23]

Should the Soviets threaten to invade, Swedish fighter pilots were ready to quickly engage and interrupt any preliminary attacks on targets such as coastal artillery installations, Berga naval base in the Stockholm archipelago, and roadside air force bases hidden across the country. "We definitely trained for that scenario all the time," says Johansson. While working at one of the air force's command centres in the late 1980s, air force officer Hanna Jungwallius noticed how "almost every week" Soviet attack aircraft would practise dropping bombs and radar-disrupting tinfoil paper strips in tandem with fighter-supported air drops of troops onto Estonia's Dagö and Ösel, both former districts of Sweden that lie only an hour from Stockholm by plane.[24]

Secret Soviet reconnaissance descriptions of Sweden helpfully identified the Swedish capital for Russian fighter pilots using formulations such as "Stockholm is easily identified from the air by virtue of its size and location between the Baltic Sea and Lake Mälaren."[25] "After the collapse of the Soviet Union, the number of Russian planes immediately fell to zero," recalls Hanna Jungwallius, who relates with amusement how a conscript once asked her during an incident readiness exercise: "Lieutenant, why are we even sitting here when there's no longer anything to see?" But these questions were never strictly theoretical because incidents that can only be described as hostile had, in fact, already been taking place in Sweden.

For several weeks during the early spring of 1984, for example, an unprecedented number of foreign conventional submarines, shallow water mini-submarines and divers were observed operating in one of Sweden's archipelagos. According to the report made by Sweden's Supreme Commander on the so-called Karlskrona Incident, which took place barely three years after the stranding of *U-137*, Swedish patrol boats, helicopters, minesweepers and land-based troops defended the Blekinge archipelago against what commanders identified as foreign enemy forces. This included a "large number of armed engagements", involving 63 hand grenades and "around fifteen or so" discharges of small arms.[26]

It is true that the Karlskrona Incident, as peace and conflict studies researcher Wilhelm Agrell notes, "was characterized by extreme confusion, major disruption of the local population's daily activities, and almost routine weapons discharges after nightfall".[27] At the same time, he points out that "Soviet intelligence was deeply interested in the Swedish coastline throughout the 1980s".[28] Lars-Erik De Geer, who worked for Sweden's National Defence Institute, speculates that these submarine incursions were also linked to Soviet efforts to plant nuclear devices in the Swedish archipelago.[29] With regard to the larger strategic context in which Sweden found itself at that time, ambassador Michael Sahlin remarks: "We were saved by the bell when the Cold War ended without the unthinkable ever taking place." In his view, the danger of Soviet invasion had only ever been greater during the 1950s: "At that time the international political system was unstable, and there was a lack of clarity about the preconditions for MAD. It was a process of action-creating-reaction with a large degree of uncertainty and in such contexts crises easily arise." The post-war decade also saw the beginnings of Sweden's secret resistance organization.

## 2

# Something Must Be Done

### "IF A COMMUNIST WON, I'D END UP IN PRISON"

As soon as World War II ended, the Soviet Union was evaluated as a potential threat to Sweden, primarily on geo-strategic grounds. The Soviet sphere of interest now encompassed Finland, the Baltic states and Poland, an area that had previously served as a buffer zone for Sweden. "In this regard the threat scenario resembled the dark years of 1940–1943, when Germany was considered capable of launching a surprise attack on Sweden directly from areas under its control," observes Agrell.[1] Resisting an attack from the east thus became the new priority for Sweden's defence planning, but it was only later that key figures in Sweden (as in other Western countries) realized the true meaning of Soviet power that lay behind its rulers' talk of peace and democracy.[2] One of them was Tage Erlander, who in the autumn of 1946 had begun his almost 25-year tenure as Social Democratic Prime Minister. Despite having celebrated the Russian Revolution in 1917 and taken inspiration from Swedish communist theories in the 1920s, he was to become fiercely anti-communist.

Ingvar Carlsson, who began working for Erlander in the Prime Minister's Office in 1958 and himself later headed several Social Democratic governments, tells the following story:

> Just before a debate with the communist leader Hilding Hagberg in the party's northern stronghold in Malmberget, Erlander was asked at the press conference whether he would rather vote for a conservative or a communist. Quick as a flash Erlander replied: "For a conservative, of course. Because then I would become leader of the opposition and then come back as prime minister, assuming that I won the next election. But if a communist won, I'd end up in prison or, in the worst case, be killed."[3]

The incident "accurately mirrors the degree to which Erlander and the vast majority of Social Democrats regarded the communists as their main enemy," observes Carlsson, and adds: "It was a question of democracy." During the 1948 election campaign, Erlander made a similar reply to Sven Linderot, who had been leader of the Moscow-controlled Swedish Communist Party since 1929 and was succeeded by Hagberg, this time stating that he expected to be confined to Sweden's equivalent of Alcatraz: "Should Mr Linderot win the election, I will likely find it very uncomfortable having to work from Långholmen Prison."[4]

---

Erlander's view of communism and its Soviet incarnation was profoundly shaped by the Polish parliamentary election of January 1947, the country's first since the outbreak of the war.[5] The terms of the Yalta Treaty between Western leaders and Joseph Stalin had stipulated that the election should be free and fair. According to the Swedish press, the election, which returned the Soviet-supported regime with a substantial majority, had been properly conducted. However, Polish telegrams that Sweden's National Defence Radio Establishment (FRA), responsible for collecting signals intelligence, decoded and presented to Erlander showed that widespread violence and voter intimidation had taken place. As historian Michael Fredholm notes, "The telegrams contained orders to the security forces to ensure that anyone arriving at a polling station was not secretly carrying a ballot paper for the opposition."[6] Shaken, Erlander recorded in his diary: "Pretty clear from his report how critical if not hostile Andersson from FRA is towards the Soviet Union. Hard to disagree after today's nasty surprise."[7]

Erlander's antipathy towards the USSR was reinforced by two events in 1948. The first was the Prague coup of February 1948, in which Czechoslovakia's Soviet-backed Communist Party seized power. The second was Stalin's "suggestion" to Finnish president Juho Paasikivi, made just hours after the coup in Czechoslovakia, that Finland's national security should be tied to that of the Soviet Union by a so-called Treaty of Friendship, Cooperation and Mutual Assistance.[8] Erlander's fears for his own country seem to have deepened accordingly. In early March, the Swedish premier recorded in his diary that he had heard rumours that plans for an impending Soviet attack on Scandinavia had received the support of domestic coup plotters: "The whole thing sounds utterly far-fetched but the behaviour of the communist parties both here and in Finland is very ominous. If the Russians convince themselves of the inevitability of war, I can well imagine that it might be better to have the conflict now rather than later."[9]

A few months later, in the middle of June 1948, Erlander received a similar "peculiar warning about an invasion of Scandinavia" from the FRA, which believed it had observed Soviet troops massing. "Is it possible that they are planning something?" the Prime Minister wondered.[10] Although war did not break out, the Soviet threat continued to loom large, and not only for Erlander and his government. Across society there was a widespread feeling that Sweden was in a vulnerable situation and that "something had to be done". In response, a number of individuals had begun to sketch the outlines of a Swedish resistance organization that could be activated if, or when, the country found itself occupied.

## HOMELAND STEWARDSHIP

There had been several initiatives along these lines in Sweden during World War II, when many people feared or even expected a German invasion. Economist Assar Lindbeck grew up near the northerly port of Luleå, which supplied Germany's arms industry with iron ore, and in his memoirs he relates how he was awakened one winter's night by his father, who had it on good authority that "German paratroopers had landed on the ice of the southern bay".[11]

These defence initiatives included the Tuesday Club, a bipartisan and clandestine anti-Nazi discussion group whose members included leading cultural figures. It would help to lay the foundation for a civilian resistance organization. The Club's founder, artist and author Amelie Posse, envisioned a national network of cells organized by the Tuesday Club, which in peacetime would report on Nazi propaganda and suspected fifth columnists, and in the event of a German occupation would "draw steel" for Sweden.[12] The Club got hold of illegal radio transmitters and distributed them so that its planned resistance groups could stay in contact during an occupation.

Similar ideas were discussed within the labour movement. In 1940, the same year as the Tuesday Club was formed, the researchers Gunnar and Alva Myrdal urged Per Albin Hansson, the Social Democratic Prime Minister of the coalition government, to create a resistance organization based on the local branches of the Social Democratic Party and the Trade Union Confederation.[13] Plans were also made for a resistance organization by the backers of a far-left newspaper: "We shall fight like guerrillas," its chief editor, Carl Johan Björklund, declared to the author Ivar Lo-Johansson.[14] In 1941, trade union representatives gathered in the cellar of the Trade Union Confederation's central Stockholm headquarters, a fortress-like building designed by Ferdinand Boberg, in order to practise with small arms in preparation for a German invasion. The group included Gunnar Sträng, chair of the Swedish Agricultural Workers' Union and subsequently a long-serving Social Democratic Minister of Finance.[15] As late as 2023, it was still possible to view the room used for storing guns and the old firing range with what appear to be bullet holes in its walls.

---

A more serious initiative was taken by C Bureau, the precursor to the intelligence service T Bureau. This was the so-called Homeland Stewardship entity, which fell under the "group organizations" that C Bureau administered along the border with occupied Norway. The group organizations, which were intended to operate as a local intelligence service that would provide advance warning of German invasion preparations, had two branches: a "tourist organization" that operated on the Norwegian side of the border, and "homeland stewards" in Sweden.[16]

Homeland stewardship was the right name for the activities of these groups.[17] In peacetime, their members were responsible for investigating suspicious individuals and vehicles, interrogating deserters and refugees, and analysing the relative strengths of German versus Swedish troop units using information supplied by the tourist organization. However, as author Gellert Hardi-Kovacs explains, in the event of a German occupation, they would re-form into a resistance organization "whose primary mission would be surveillance and sabotage of the enemy's supply lines".[18] Selected "homeland houses" would become bases of operation and weapon depots. The organization recruited individuals, such as local businessmen, whose jobs offered a pretext for regularly crossing the border as well as the opportunity for remaining on Swedish soil following an occupation. C Bureau placed exacting demands on personal reliability, "strong nerves, endurance, and the ability to observe".[19] Its agents referred to each other by codenames and had only limited information about the organization's structure.

It is unclear to what extent these plans were realized. Hardi-Kovacs thinks that they were "likely never implemented along the entire border".[20] What is more, until now it has also been unclear what became of the Homeland Stewardship entity after the end of the war.[21] The fact that homeland stewards apparently existed as early as 1940 is interesting given that the official Swedish view of partisans and resistance groups was uniformly negative – a type of warfare, as historian Henrik Berggren explains, "that was regarded as dishonourable if not outright criminal".[22,23]

It was at around this time that Prime Minister Hansson had rejected the Myrdals' proposal for a Social Democratic-led resistance organization on the grounds that, were the existence of such an organization to leak out, it could be seen as an expression of defeatism or lack of faith in Sweden's conventional military forces.[24] Not until January 1943 did Hansson make public a directive from Sweden's government and military high command – a directive that remains in force to this day – instructing the entire population to resist at all costs. The newspaper *Dagens Nyheter* called it "Sweden's watchword", and argued that the experience of other countries showed that citizens must be prepared to resist.[25] In Denmark and Norway, the occupied countries closest to Sweden, no preparations had been made and organized resistance to the Germans was initially slow.

This situation was precisely what the various parties behind the formation of Sweden's resistance organizations in the early 1940s were hoping to avoid. Amelie Posse saw Germany's occupation of Czechoslovakia, her home until 1939, as highly instructive. As she asked rhetorically in her address to the first meeting of the Tuesday Club: "Think how much easier it would have been for the Czech people if, when the Germans invaded, their country had already created a functioning and thoroughly prepared resistance organization? If only some far-sighted and responsible citizens had managed to create an apparatus that could be activated when needed."[26] The same question would be asked by other Swedes as the Cold War got under way.

## "PREPARING AN UNDERGROUND ORGANIZATION"

In May 1947, Torsten Nothin, a grand old man of the Social Democrats who at that time was Stockholm's governor and thus also its most senior police officer, submitted a memorandum on Sweden's defence marked "Highly Confidential" to Prime Minister Erlander. In it, Nothin presented the following argument:

> Even during peacetime [...] it is imperative to make plans for an active resistance organization, for which purposes should be appointed suitable leaders whose names should not be made public. Only after an occupation, whether partial or total, when the resistance organization has been activated, can its various local heads, who until that point need know only their joint commanders, be allowed to make their existence known to their preassigned collaborators and set them to work. These arrangements will allow a resistance organization to be quickly established and ensure that its operations are directed by individuals whose trustworthiness has already been calmly evaluated and determined during peacetime.[27]

When, exactly two years later, Nothin again contacted the prime minster about the possibility of establishing a resistance organization, it is likely that his plans were far more developed.

As Erlander noted in his diary: "Last Monday I met with Nothin, who explained his plans for a wartime partisan organization. He is probably right."[28]

It might seem strange that Erlander, who is best known to posterity as one of the architects of Sweden's welfare state and for his famous appearance on a popular late-night talk show programme, was involved in planning a covert resistance organization. In fact, he was ideally suited to such work. During the war, Erlander had worked first as Secretary of State for Social Affairs and then as Deputy Minister of Social Affairs, where his responsibilities included the Swedish security service and the training of Danish and Norwegian so-called police troops, who would take control of their respective countries after a German withdrawal. The Ministry of Social Affairs also had directed the delivery of arms and other kinds of assistance to the Danish and Norwegian resistance organizations.[29] Together with Olof Palme and Carl Bildt, Erlander was one of the few Swedish prime ministers who regularly requested and received briefings from representatives of the intelligence services.[30] Sven Aspling, who served under Erlander as secretary of the Social Democratic Party, may have been justified in calling him "the biggest intelligence guy of them all".[31]

During the war, Erlander had himself speculated vaguely about creating a resistance organization under the direction of Gunnar Sträng. "Because I was chair of the Agricultural Workers' Union, I would be given a role," recalled Sträng in 1992: "I replied that I was ready to serve but then I heard no more about it."[32] In the 1940s, the Agricultural Workers' Union had almost 40,000 members, who were highly knowledgeable about their local communities and absolutely central to the supply of foodstuffs during wartime.[33] Erlander was therefore both well informed and receptive to new ideas when he was approached in summer 1949 with plans for a resistance organization. On this occasion he presumably met with not just Nothin but also Anders Grafström, a captain in the Defence Staff and adjutant to Chief of the Army Carl August Ehrensvärd.

As early as 1947, while Ehrensvärd was Chief of the Defence Staff, he and Grafström had initiated a project for a resistance organization. They had informed Defence Minister Allan Vougt and Interior Minister Eije Mossberg, who were both positive.[34] However, Thede Palm, the head of the intelligence service T Bureau and, by virtue of his meticulously detailed diaries, a key witness to events described later in this book, recorded that the proposal was temporarily shelved because of a lack of interest from Nils Swedlund, Ehrensvärd's successor as Chief of the Defence Staff. "Now Grafström has brought it up again and pitched it to Erlander, who gave his approval," noted Palm in his diary in early June 1949, adding that Nothin would also "be involved, but quite separately from his role as a defence investigator".[35]

Palm was referring to the fact that Nothin had recently been appointed chair of a wide-ranging parliamentary inquiry intended to provide a "full overview" of the nation's defences.[36] However, as Nothin saw it, the resistance organization lay outside of the inquiry's remit. Accordingly, he did not discuss the matter with the members of the inquiry committee, which included future conservative leader Jarl Hjalmarson. Nor did Nothin speak with Helge Jung, Supreme Commander, despite having made repeated reassurances that they would work together very closely, or with Allan Vougt.[37] Instead, he went directly to Erlander.[38] As the Supreme Commander himself remarked: "Despite not having been properly briefed [by the military leadership], Nothin has gone ahead with preparing an underground organization."[39]

It may be that Grafström and Ehrensvärd, both military men, had thrown in their lot with Nothin. But in that case the trio's plan was not the only option on the table. Thede Palm himself had also considered "a special organization that would be activated by an occupation" and had even heard rumours that "something similar was being prepared by the Trade Union Confederation".[40]

It would appear that these various initiatives were consolidated and concretized into a single organization that remained operational until the 1990s. In the following section I will present the first participants in this resistance organization. Let us call them "the men of 1949".

# PART TWO

# The Men of 1949

# 3

# The Top Brass

## THE SEXTUPLETS

On 20 June 1949, Tage Erlander issued four letters of authorization using the prime minister's own stationery. Each was written by hand and worded identically: "I hereby commission you, together with others whom I have appointed, to form a committee for the purposes of planning a resistance organization that shall become active in the event of any part of this country being occupied by a foreign power." These letters of authorization are critical documents for the present study in that they establish that from a very early stage the resistance organization had a democratic basis, albeit a weak one.

Strictly speaking, the documents signed by the Prime Minister on that day lacked legal and constitutional legitimacy under the constitution then in force – Sweden's so-called Instrument of Government of 1809 – which stipulated that decisions could only be formally adopted by the government in council with the King as chairman. However, Björn von Sydow, a political scientist who helped Erlander write his memoirs in the early 1970s and became Speaker of the Swedish Parliament in the early 2000s, does not exclude the possibility that "a practice had been established for this kind of unusual communication in certain situations", which either had the King's approval or was the result of legal deliberations within the Government Office.[1] As von Sydow remarks:

> In the situation in which Sweden found itself during the Second World War and now the Cold War, when an attack was feared, it may have been thought that the general authority held by the Prime Minister – then and now – sufficed for him to be able to take measures that possibly lacked a precise legal basis. At that time, the Social Democrats were in government and had an absolute majority in the Lower Chamber and almost a majority in the Upper Chamber. There was thus a very powerful democratic underpinning for the actions of Erlander's government.

The procedure certainly followed Erlander's own view of governmental powers, namely that governments which enjoyed a parliamentary majority should show initiative and willingness to act.[2] However, as von Sydow notes, there was also the fact that King Gustaf V was "extremely frail". The King's physical and psychological health, which was indeed failing, is described at length in Erlander's diaries. As far back as the formal opening of parliament in January 1946, Erlander had "felt that this ceremony would be the last in which he [the King] participated".[3]

Three years later, in December 1949, Birger Ekeberg, the Marshal of the Realm, Herman Zetterberg, the Minister of Justice, and the Prime Minister himself described as "an appalling prospect, both for the monarch and the monarchy" the possibility that Gustaf V might officiate at next year's opening of parliament, including presenting the government's new policy programme in his King's Speech (a plan he ultimately abandoned).[4] In council with the government just a few weeks later, in January 1950, the King seemed to Erlander to be "obviously confused".[5] More than once, Erlander was convinced that the end was near for the King, an inevitability that troubled him and the other members of the cabinet. "They were anxious about his successor, Prince Gustaf Adolf," notes von Sydow.

Erlander's diary makes repeated reference to the unease felt in government circles about the future Gustav VI Adolf. "Talking to the King is as pleasant as dealing with the Crown Prince is awful," reads one particularly striking entry from October 1946.[6] Among his other character flaws, Gustaf Adolf was regarded as petty and prone to interfering. Indeed, according to Björn von Sydow, Gustaf V's health and the likelihood – or, as the cabinet ministers saw it, risk – of the Crown Prince suddenly succeeding to the throne may well have influenced the decision to exclude the Council of State from involvement in the sensitive matter of establishing a Swedish resistance organization.

This hypothesis finds support in one of Erlander's diary entries from September 1950, a month before the King's death. It summarizes a discussion among members of the cabinet about whether it was appropriate, given the tense global situation following North Korea's attack on South Korea that summer, which was widely regarded as the harbinger of a Communist invasion of NATO's border with West Germany, that Gustaf V abdicate in favour of Crown Prince Gustaf Adolf.[7]

In his diary Erlander wrote: "At today's cabinet coffee meeting I relayed [Torsten] Nothin's opinion that, if matters become very critical, it will be more stable to have the King stay on, because the government will then be able to proceed without unnecessary interference. [Finance Minister Per Edvin] Sköld thought that these were wise words and laughed heartily."[8,9] The cabinet's prediction was confirmed later that year when the new King, to the fury of Foreign Minister Östen Undén, presented his own draft of the King's Speech – formally speaking, a statement issued by the government – in which he sought to emphasize "the gravity of the situation".[10]

It would take several years before Erlander and Gustaf VI Adolf enjoyed what von Sydow calls "a close and trusting relationship".[11] This improved relationship likely made possible the strengthening of the resistance organization's legal status. At this point, however, in the summer of 1949, the only official sanction given to the organization was Erlander's letters of authorization.

---

The recipients of the Prime Minister's letters of authorization were to form a "company board" for the resistance organization.[12] Answerable to this "group of superior and high-society individuals", as former intelligence chief Thede Palm ironically described it to the Neutrality Policy Commission in 1993, were himself and two other men on a "more operative" level: Anders Grafström and someone whom Palm did not identity.[13] I will return to this trio shortly and introduce the third man, insurance company executive Elov Bergkvist.

We may conclude that the "superior" figures on the board were originally five in number, given that Palm's diary entries up until summer 1950 referred to the group as "the quintuplets".[14] Yet Erlander had issued only four letters of authorization, which were addressed to the following: Alvar Lindencrona, an insurance company director; Carl August Erhensvärd, Chief of the Army; Håkan Sterky, director-general of the telecommunications authority; and Anders E. Bjelle, at the time an influential figure within the Swedish Agricultural Federation.[15] It seems likely that the fifth board member was someone who, perhaps by virtue of his professional position, did not require authorization by the Prime Minister. That person was Eije Mossberg, Erlander's Minister of the Interior. According to a handwritten and signed letter to the Neutrality Policy Commission, Mossberg was "instructed by Erlander to follow and oversee the planning and implementation of the general guidelines for the work", a commission that Mossberg carried out during the remainder of his time in post and that he "verbally returned [...] to him [Erlander]" when he retired from government in 1951.[16]

It is worth pausing for a moment at the word *verbally*, which would be redundant were it not for the fact that the other board members had received their commission in writing and were expected to return it in the same form. Thus we find that Anders E. Bjelle's personal authorization is attached to a note, dated 22 June 1949, two days *after* the date of the letter of authorization itself, stipulating that: "In the event of its owner's [i.e. Bjelle's] death, this document must be returned to Prime Minister Tage Erlander." This directive seems to have been followed, since both it and the two other letters of authorization that would have been returned during Erlander's tenure as Prime Minister – namely those belonging to Ehrensvärd and Sterky – are preserved in the Erlander Collection of the Swedish Labour Movement's Archives and Library.[17]

During the final stages of World War II, Mossberg had succeeded Erlander first as State Secretary for Social Affairs and later as Deputy Minister. He was therefore accustomed to working with sensitive issues as well as with Erlander himself. Mossberg had also shown the keenest interest when, in 1947, Ehrensvärd and Grafström had approached him and Allan Vougt (who was seen as untrustworthy in defence circles) with plans for a resistance organization. Then, in 1949, Mossberg had lent his support to Nothin's initiative for an underground movement.[18] When we additionally consider that Thede Palm, after his first meeting in November 1949 with the members of what he called "the assembled commission", noted that an unnamed cabinet minister had chaired the meeting, it becomes difficult to see how the fifth member of the board could be anyone but Mossberg.[19]

For final confirmation, we can turn to the diary that Helge Jung kept while Supreme Commander. An entry made in September 1949 states that Ehrensvärd briefed Jung "on a meeting with Mossberg, Sterky, Bjelle, Lindencrona, and Grafström [who had operative responsibility] at the home of E-d [Ehrensvärd]".[20] However, an entry in Thede Palm's diary for June 1950 mentions "a meeting with the five big players at which the sixth was also present", after which he refers to "the sextuplets".[21] This coded designation for the board, which also appears in the diary kept by Helge Jung while Supreme Commander, was in use until at least summer 1966 when Palm left his operative role in the resistance organization.[22]

We can therefore say with confidence that the composition of the board had grown from five to six seats by summer 1950. This most likely took place with Erlander's approval in light of the fact that six months earlier, according to Palm, the committee had considered sending the Prime Minister "a request to be assigned an additional man".[23] As with the Swedish Academy, a seat on the committee could occasionally fall vacant, prompting a new appointment. After voluntarily leaving the resistance organization in 1951, Ehrensvärd was succeeded by Supreme Commander Nils Swedlund. After Bjelle died in 1961, he was replaced by Bertil Kugelberg, head of the Employers' Confederation, who was in turn succeeded by Curt-Steffan Giesecke in 1966 as part of a change of leadership in the Confederation. The sixth seat on the board of the resistance organization was initially offered to Arne Geijer, who in 1950 had not yet become head of the Trade Union Confederation but was still head of the Swedish Metalworkers' Union. Although I will substantiate this claim in the following account of the sextuplets, it goes without saying that a detailed description of each and every member of the board is neither practical nor necessary. It likewise makes most sense to begin with the group's most important member.

## WILD MAN

Given the importance of the role played by the Social Democratic official Torsten Nothin in the founding of the resistance organization, it would have been natural for him to have taken a leading role in its development. On the contrary, however, he seems to have more or less withdrawn from its activities after June 1949. Instead, the role of *primus inter pares* on the organization's board fell to Alvar Lindencrona, director of the insurance company

Thule. Lindencrona's letter of authorization was identical to the others in all but one regard: it would be "confirmed", more than 20 years later, by the signature of Prime Minister Olof Palme.[24] In December 1949, Lindencrona explained to Thede Palm, who held a position in the organization immediately below the level of board member, that he, Lindencrona, would "serve as a kind of managing director".[25]

In his diary, Palm referred to Lindencrona by the codename "Wild Man", a figure in Northern European mythology who is typically depicted as heavy, hirsute and armed with a club. I can confirm that this somewhat unflattering codename refers to Lindencrona because I have correlated his pocket calendars with Palm's diary and established that the "Wild Man" and Lindencrona were present in the same places on the same dates.[26] The same is true of Lindencrona and the individual who was later designated by the similar codename "Shaggy Man", often shortened to "S.M."

These codenames may have been inspired either by Lindencrona's curly hair, of which he was apparently immensely proud, or – perhaps more likely – by the mythological Wild Man's abode: the fairy realm of Ultima Thule on civilization's northernmost fringe.* "Wild Man" could thus be translated as "Man of Thule". Palm, who was a historian of religion, may have come to feel that the code was a little too obvious and changed it to "Shaggy Man". Or perhaps codenames evolve organically, as nicknames for children often do. Were it needed, further confirmation can be found in correspondence between Grafström and Ehrensvärd in the 1960s in which the "Shaggy Man" is mentioned in the context of a merger between the insurance companies Skandia and Thule.[27]

Eric Krönmark, who served as the resistance organization's contact person in the centre-right coalition governments of the 1970s, describes Lindencrona's role as "really a combination of board chairman and managing director" in that he chaired

*Appropriately enough, a wild man is featured on the heraldic shield of Lappland, Sweden's most northerly region.

the meetings of its steering committee but also had operative responsibility. This combination, according to Krönmark, suited Lindencrona well: "He had a [civilian] position that did not make him a person of interest for an occupying power." What is more, Krönmark remembers personally attending the meetings of the resistance organization's board but without the knowledge of Prime Minister Thorbjörn Fälldin: "I did not inform him. I treated this as top secret and assumed that [outgoing Prime Minister] Palme had briefed Fälldin on the resistance organization."*

This marked a departure from the resistance organization's early years, when Lindencrona had reported to the Prime Minster personally on the progress of the underground activities. At that time Ingvar Carlsson had an office across the hall from Tage Erlander's room in the Prime Minister's Office, a tiny unit with only five employees, and could therefore observe that occasionally meetings took place "between Lindencrona and Erlander with no one else present". The meetings seem to have caused some puzzlement to the young political secretary. "Eventually," Carlsson recalls, "it became clear to me that they related to plans for a resistance organization should Sweden ever be occupied." He remembers that it was either Olof Palme, at that time Erlander's foreign and security policy advisor, or the Prime Minister himself who told him the reason for Lindencrona's visits.

---

It might seem like a contradiction that a blue-blooded aristocrat, whose family were ennobled by Queen Ulrika Eleonora in 1719, should have agreed to be the leader of a resistance organization

*In fact, Olof Palme had *not* informed Thorbjörn Fälldin about the existence of the resistance organization by the time of the change of government in 1976. The information was instead communicated by Supreme Commander Stig Synnergren.

during the 1940s, when Sweden was completely dominated by the Social Democratic party. And yet, as Lindencrona's eldest daughter, Elisabeth Lindencrona Paues, explains, her father, like many of his generation in the Swedish nobility, regarded it as a duty to serve, if necessary "by giving their life for their country".[28] His son, Gustaf Lindencrona, echoes this view: "Father was above all else a man of conscience and a patriot. He spoke warmly about Sweden and the needs of the country."[29]

During the war, Alvar Lindencrona had served in the Ministry of Defence under Per Edvin Sköld, whom Gustaf Lindencrona remembers his father admiring greatly, and the Ministry of Communications. He later became a divisional director at the Swedish Civil Aviation Administration, where his duties, according to an obituary penned by his friend Rolf af Klintberg, involved "flying around the world and negotiating the international aviation treaties that formed the basis for a huge expansion of Swedish air traffic".[30]

Accepting a secret commission for the government would have come naturally to a man with Lindencrona's background. Like many others in the insurance business, he probably had both an aptitude for and an interest in using past experiences to predict and pre-empt the various risks to which the mass of people are exposed. He was likely aware, too, of the importance of maximizing damage limitation and re-establishing normal conditions if disaster should indeed strike.

There is also another, less visible aspect to this connection. In a speech given to the Swedish Insurance Society on the occasion of its centenary in 1975, Prime Minister Olof Palme, whose own father and grandfather had been managers of the Thule insurance company for many years, declared that the social-democratic welfare state and insurance companies had a common goal, namely to minimize the material costs entailed by accidents and poor public health. Palme noted the insurance industry's contributions in this area: "From my time as Minister of Communications, I remember campaigns against drink-driving, for safety belts, against night-time accidents, for child safety, and many others [...] which were coordinated with the various popular movements of the day."[31] One way to view the resistance organization – a perspective that is underscored by the fact that Lindencrona was chairman of the quasi-governmental National Society for Road Safety, a post he inherited from Torsten Nothin – is that it represented an extension of these kinds of behaviour-modifying initiatives and collaborations between the public sector, insurance companies and special interest organizations.

As a boy, Lindencrona had strongly identified with the Scarlet Pimpernel, a fictional aristocrat who rescues French noblemen and their families from the guillotine during the Reign of Terror by bringing them to England. Elisabeth Lindencrona Paues speculates that Baroness Orczy's hero may even have inspired her father's decision to become involved in a Swedish resistance organization. In passing, she mentions that a relative of her husband, Staffan Paues, also saw the Scarlet Pimpernel as a role model. A contemporary of Alvar Lindencrona, he was the businessman and diplomat Raoul Wallenberg.[32]

Admittedly, it might seem paradoxical that Lindencrona should have been the leader of a resistance organization founded largely on the initiative of leading Social Democrats. Not only did he have an aristocratic background, he actively cultivated a patrician aura by wearing a large signet ring and white spats. His daughter remembers him fondly as a "dandy".[33] And yet, as the artist (and baron) Carl Johan De Geer rightly observed in a TV programme in 1991, "this cover was absolutely perfect".[34] While a teenager in the 1950s, De Geer had regularly visited the Lindencrona family home, often accompanied Alvar Lindencrona in their chauffeur-driven black Mercedes, and regarded him as the "embodiment of patriarchal tradition and joviality".

At the same time, this was perhaps a cover in a double sense. Beneath Lindencrona's upper-class veneer lay not just a secret resistance agent but a precursor of a more progressive era. In February 1947, while still only 36, he had been appointed managing director of Thule. From his executive suite in Thule's modern headquarters on Sveavägen 44 in Stockholm – "Sweden's first 'scientific offices' with the latest new-fangled inventions such as air conditioning, noise-absorbing walls, and standardized office furniture" – he implemented an array of groundbreaking changes.[35] Long before Bror Rexed, director of the National Swedish Board of Health in the late 1960s, directed his staff to stop using the formal pronoun *ni* (the Swedish equivalent to *vous* in French or *Sie* in German), Lindencrona was addressing his employees in all settings by the informal pronoun *du*.

This informal mode of address quickly spread through the firm. According to the memoirs of Lennart Grundborn, a self-styled "Thule-ite", it was a key factor in the "Thule spirit" of positivity and inclusiveness that permeated the insurance company under Lindencrona's leadership.[36] He created an American-style junior board in order to give primarily younger staff members a forum in which to discuss the issues being faced by the regular board and to present new ideas to the management.

For the benefit of a larger community, Lindencrona created the so-called Thule School, which offered ambitious young women whose formal education had stopped at 14 a relatively broad – and, not least, paid – three-year training programme that introduced them to professional life while also promoting social mobility. The Thule School, according to a newspaper article published on its decennial in 1957, had from its inception been "something of an experiment", but its success was undeniable.[37] Other similar social initiatives in which Lindencrona had a hand included the Thule Home, an early and ambitious model for retirement housing near Lund in southern Sweden, and central Stockholm's first medical group practice, which Thule jointly established with the Stockholm Doctors' Association.[38]

Lindencrona would today be described as an exemplar of corporate social responsibility. Much of his energy doubtless came from a desire to prevent a nationalization of the Swedish insurance industry, which was an entirely plausible scenario when he took up his post as Thule's managing director in 1947.

As the leading Social Democratic newspaper *Morgon-Tidningen* wrote that year: "the large financial interests within the insurance industry must prepare for closer scrutiny of how necessary their business is for Sweden's welfare state."[39] As Lindencrona demonstrated with Thule's various activities, private insurance companies did not have to be treated as obstacles to the emerging welfare state but could rather be seen as complements to it, in accordance with the socially beneficial and cooperative origins of insurance itself. At the same time, Lindencrona himself seems to have been prompted by a genuine sense of social responsibility.

With the passing of the years, Lindencrona came to be seen, in the words of his employee Lennart Grundborn, as "a forceful and visionary business leader and a key figure in the insurance business as a whole".[40] He was nonetheless forced to resign as director in the mid-1960s when Thule merged with its rival, Skandia. The reason why Lindencrona was not invited to lead the new corporate entity was his failed investment in securing for Thule a recovery organization, one of whose planned functions was offering roadside assistance to the company's car-owning customers. According to Thede Palm, who was unexpectedly offered a seat on the board of the new recovery organization, Lindencrona had wanted "it to be a non-profit company with a social basis".[41] He was instead nominated to the board of Skandia.[42] "A little leak will sink a great ship," observes Gustaf Lindencrona of his father's dismissal: "A very sad affair."

Alvar Lindencrona nonetheless remained an influential figure within Swedish industry, holding board positions for companies such as the car and aircraft manufacturer SAAB and its international subsidiaries. He wound up his career in the late 1970s by accepting a nomination to the post of deputy director of the ICC International Court of Arbitration in Paris, an organization in which he had already served for some years as chairman of its national committee in Sweden. The numerous positions which he held on the boards of various associations towards the end of his life included deputy director of the House of Nobility. By Lindencrona's own admission, this would have amused his mother, Ingeborg Lindencrona (née Jegerhjelm, a noble family name), who "never really approved of [his] career in commerce".[43]

---

Lindencrona's "special assignment for the defence forces", as former Chief of the Army Carl Eric Almgren cryptically put it in an obituary for his former comrade in the resistance organization, remained unknown to his family until shortly before Lindencrona's sudden death of complications from angina in December 1981.[44] As his son Gustaf recalls: "Father, who was in hospital, said, 'I just want to tell you that I have been running an enterprise in the national interest.' I thought that it was strange but also admirable and that I should have realized earlier, but I never did." The truth of his father's surprising confession seemed to be confirmed to Gustaf a few days later when a representative from the armed forces called at the family's home in central Stockholm, presented his credentials, and requested to be allowed to remove a "huge black box", together with its unknown contents, from the locked safe that Alvar Lindencrona had had installed in the apartment.

By 1978, after almost 30 years as leader of the resistance organization, Lindencrona was forced by his advanced age and declining health to tender his resignation to Minister of Defence Eric Krönmark, who also recalls that the organization's board was permitted to hold meetings in Skandia's own headquarters. Clearly, Lindencrona had held onto documents or some kind of equipment connected with the assignment. One possibility is that the item in question was the personal letter of authorization that had been signed by Tage Erlander and Olof Palme; an equivalent document belonging to board member Anders E. Bjelle, it will be recalled, included the stipulation that it be returned "in the event of its owner's death".[45]

While growing up, Lindencrona's son Gustaf had remained largely oblivious to his father's secret life, noting only that he often held meetings in the family's spacious apartment with famous individuals such as Carl August Ehrensvärd, Tage Erlander and Minister of the Interior Gunnar Hedlund. Yet Gustaf's study trip to the Soviet Union in 1961 caused considerable but unexplained anxiety at home. "Father was very doubtful about whether I should make the trip. At the time I did not understand why, but of course it's quite clear now," he recalls.

His sister, Elisabeth Lindencrona Paues, had a different experience. According to Ole Grøn and military historian Michael Clemmesen, it was not unusual in Denmark's civil resistance and intelligence networks for "the role of agent to be handed down from individual farmer or tradesman to their eldest son".[46] When there were several siblings, a single child was typically selected to ensure continuity of the network.[47] Something similar, if not quite the same, happened to Elisabeth Lindencrona Paues.[48] During her younger years and as an adult, she helped her father by accompanying him on trips relating to the resistance organization in Sweden and abroad, her presence making them seem like normal family excursions. She was presumably chosen to carry out this assignment – unwittingly – because of her considerable social skills. "I was very confident and not afraid of anyone," Elisabeth remembers. "I could talk to 'Uncle Dodde' [the financier Marcus Wallenberg] quite naturally."

In a letter to Elisabeth's father-in-law, Johan Paues, from December 1973, Alvar Lindencrona described his daughter's social talent, which had recently been demonstrated at a dinner in Paris for the wives of the former presidents of the International Chamber of Commerce: "She had been so charming that the chaps made a point of coming up afterwards to tell me how delighted their wives had been."[49] In light of this, it is probably not surprising, and also quite appropriate, that Elisabeth learned of her father's assignment before her siblings did, during his final summer. In strict confidence, and in reply to the many searching questions about his activities during their many journeys over the years, Lindencrona told her that he had been working covertly for his country and had had a special responsibility for the safety of the royal family in the event of war. If an attack came, Elisabeth recalls, "The whole family was to board a plane, whose engines were kept running at all times, that would transport him and the royal family to southern England."

Another person who would likely have boarded the plane was Astrid Tunell, who loyally worked as Alvar Lindencrona's secretary for almost her entire professional life. She, too, was part of the resistance organization's inner circle, as is confirmed by her daughter, Ingrid Rosander, who personally knew "Uncle Alvar" and often played with the Lindencrona children.[50] When hotelier and regional commander Reinhold Geijer, whom Ingrid Rosander's mother knew as simply "Regi", revealed his involvement in the resistance organization in the mid-1990s, Astrid Tunell also decided to lift the veil of secrecy. Rosander recalls her tearful words: "'You should know, Ingrid, that if a foreign power had invaded us, there was a plane at Bromma airport ready to take off with the royal family and the Lindencrona family, and that there would also have been room in that plane for you and me.'" Rosander's account is all the more credible because she is the only person to have named Bromma airport in this connection.

Ingrid Rosander's and Elisabeth Lindencrona Paues's matching accounts of how they and Alvar Lindencrona would have been flown to a major NATO country have the ring of truth. This view is echoed by Ingemar Engman, who in the mid-1960s not only sat on the board of the Social Democratic Youth League (SSU) but also worked as an analyst for the intelligence service IB before becoming – to put it somewhat euphemistically – a civil servant at the Ministry of Defence. According to P. G. Vinge, former head of the Swedish security service, Engman was "one of the very top people at the Ministry of Defence" and "the person who was effectively in charge of the Viggen [fighter jet] project in the Government Building".[51]

Ingemar Engman gained a general insight into the resistance movement by cultivating a very close personal relationship to IB director Birger Elmér and Supreme Commander Stig Synnergren, who both "wanted to inform a junior Social Democrat" about what was taking place in the deep state.[52] At the Ministry of Defence, Engman was in charge of state financial support for the organization, which during his tenure came from the Defence Staff's budget for secret operations and was supplemented by "ad hoc private money" from financiers in the private business sector.

According to Engman, Lindencrona would indeed have been stationed in southern England in the event of war: "A wartime HQ had been prepared, not only for him but for everyone [in the planned administration in exile]. Olof Palme once visited it in person."[53] Just as the Chief of the Navy, if invasion was imminent, would "disappear to England" and organize conventional military operations as a kind of "Supreme Commander in exile", Lindencrona would direct the civil resistance struggle from the wartime HQ. "It was the same idea but they [the Chief of the Navy and Lindencrona] had completely different tasks," explains Engman, adding that if necessary another person would have been appointed to lead the resistance on the ground in occupied Sweden.

Providing the government in exile with intelligence on what was happening on Swedish territory was "part of the mission", noted Curt-Steffan Giesecke, Lindencrona's successor.[54] Additional details are provided by Eric Krönmark: "Moving the King to England was a given. He would likely have been accompanied by five ministers, as would be required for the government in exile to be able to adopt legal decisions." Krönmark claims to have been unaware that Lindencrona's resistance organization had responsibility for protecting the royal family. This anomaly can be explained, however, by the fact that this task was at some point transferred to another, unknown organization. "My understanding is that Lindencrona's committee was initially responsible for the royal family," says Engman: "But the task was subsequently divided up, and I am not entirely sure who eventually assumed responsibility." Krönmark's account was also echoed by Giesecke.[55]

According to Carl Kleman, an industrialist, officer in the reserve, and close friend since childhood of Sweden's current monarch, King Carl XVI Gustaf, responsibility for evacuating the royal family in the event of an invasion lay with a number of prominent noblemen, all of whom had a background as cavalry captains:

> Gösta Lewenhaput had been part of the Crown Prince's council ever since [his father and the heir apparent Prince] Gustaf Adolf died, and Greger Lewenhaupt, the managing director of British Petroleum's Swedish subsidiary, was intimate with the royal family, as was Carl Lewenhaupt [director of the ICA supermarket chain]. These three brothers had grown up together on Geddeholm estate outside Västerås. Sten Banér, trustee of Sjöö Castle in Uppland County, had a son who attended Sigtuna [private school] with the Crown Prince.[56]

Kleman claims that the men formed a special group that was probably called *Adelsfanan*, an aristocratic name given to Sweden's first regular cavalry unit, which had been established in the 16th century.[57]

"They were a VIP group," remembers Sten Banér's son Carl, an officer in the reserve and agronomist, who shared a room with Crown Prince Carl Gustaf at Sigtuna. "The obsequious treatment they received from [Supreme Commander] Torsten Rapp when he met them at the [Defence Staff's] 'Grey House' suggests that they had an exclusive assignment."[58] He continues:

> All that Father would say was that it involved "communications". My guess is that it had to do with how, in the event of a war, people would get about if there were cordons or if the railway were sabotaged. It could well have related to an evacuation plan and I would not be at all surprised if it involved the royal family.

Carl Banér also points out that the members of this mysterious group of cavalry captains all came from noble families with personal ties to the Swedish royal family: Banér, Lewenhaupt, Bonde, von Celsing and d'Otrante. "The only one who was not a peer was Claës Palme," he adds, "but they regarded it as a feather in their cap that they had the brother of Olof [Palme], who by the 1950s and 1960s was already an influential figure."

Whatever the case, that the Swedish resistance movement regarded getting the King out of the country as a priority is confirmed by an article published in a prominent Swedish military journal in the early 1980s, which examines the legal framework that would apply to the government, civil service and citizenry in the event of Sweden being occupied, and how these various actors would be required to behave in such a situation.[59] One of its authors was former security service head Åke Hasselrot, who, according to his deposition to Sweden's Neutrality Commission, served as a "legal consultant" to the resistance organization from the mid-1960s to the mid-1970s at the personal request of Minister of Defence Sven Andersson, Tage Erlander and Alvar Lindencrona.[60] This circumstance makes the article a key source.

As regards the government's location during occupation, the article emphasizes that while the version of the constitution then in force (the so-called Instrument of Government of 1974) gave the government the option of choosing whether to abandon Swedish territory and operate from elsewhere, in practice the government was required to do so in order to preserve its integrity and work for the country's liberation. Hasselrot and his co-author, former Chancellor of Justice Bengt Lännergren, regarded the fact that the King was legally required to follow the government in order to fulfil his duties as head of state as a blessing for the civilian resistance struggle:

> In the event of war and occupation, it can be assumed that the head of state will play a far greater role than in peacetime. The King represents the sovereign authority of the State and symbolizes the continuity of the country's

> existence as an independent nation. This relationship has a particular importance in an ancient kingdom such as Sweden.
>
> […] It is clear from [a review of historical events in occupied Denmark and Norway] that the King in both of our neighbouring countries, by fulfilling his constitutional obligations towards the democratic form of government, was able to make an effective contribution towards strengthening the resolve of the nation's people. There is every reason to assume that the King of Sweden, under comparable circumstances, would do the same.[61]

The key thing was that the Swedish population did not see relocation as a "shameful escape".[62] For that reason, argued Hasselrot and Lännergren, it was vital to establish a peacetime bipartisan agreement that the King and the government should leave the country if it were invaded by an occupying power. Such an agreement was effectively reached in the late 1980s when, as a result of reforms to the constitution, parliament and the government were both prohibited from adopting decisions in occupied territory.[63]

But how, if it were ever needed, would such an evacuation have worked in practice?

Chief of the Navy Per Rudberg has attested that, as part of his secret assignment as Supreme Commander in exile (an assignment that remained in force even after retirement), he was given access to a civilian business jet.[64] A now declassified memo also indicates that the Defence Staff in the early 1950s had plans to finance the purchase of civilian aircraft by Swedish industries key to any war effort so that they could be used for purposes such as "transporting personnel and materiel to locations far behind the front".[65] In light of these revelations, it is easy to imagine Alvar Lindencrona using a business jet to rescue the royal family and install them and himself in England for the duration of a war. He could easily have obtained an aircraft via SAAB, a company that seems to have been connected, at least indirectly, to the resistance organization and of whose governing board Lindencrona was a member for over 30 years.

Sten Gustafsson, now deceased, who in 1978 was appointed director of SAAB-Scania, has related to Lindencrona's son Gustaf that his father was put on the boards of the firm's American and British subsidiaries so as to be able to visit those countries regularly without raising suspicion. Lindencrona's son recalls the episode with amusement: "Much later someone came asking about all this, and I referred them to Sten Gustafsson. But he claimed not to know anything, which was clearly a lie."

One of probably several alternatives to using Bromma airport or some other airfield as an extraction point was the westerly port of Grundsund. Built in 1918 as what legendary Swedish troubadour Evert Taube once called "the west coast's greatest fishing harbour", it lies close to England.[66] Alvar Lindencrona's father, also called Gustaf, had initiated the project in his capacity as director of the Board for Public Road and Water Structures. As Lennart Grundborn points out, "The harbour in Grundsund occupies a strategic position on Sweden's west coast. It is sufficiently anonymous and well situated to be able to assist in the stay-behind organization's task of facilitating the escape of key individuals."[67]

Grundborn's grandfather, Lars Carlsson, was harbourmaster of Grundsund from the mid-1920s to 1948 – an official position that involved regulating Swedish harbours and ports and was the precursor of today's marine police. During this period, he got to know Gustaf Lindencrona senior and, later, his son Alvar. The latter visited Grundsund with his family several times and on at least one occasion received Carlsson at the Lindencronas' apartment in central Stockholm.[68] The strength of this friendship is indicated by the fact that, in 1952, Carlsson needed to make only a brief telephone call to Alvar Lindencrona in order for the young Lennart Grundborn to be given a job at Thule.[69]

In the summer of the following year, 1953, Minister of Defence Torsten Nilsson, via his State Secretary Olle Karleby, sent Alvar Lindencrona an "*insistent* request" to accept an assignment to personally investigate the Swedish military's regional and local site assets. While working on his report, which he managed to deliver by December, Thule's managing director paid visits to "every high command centre, a number of regional military centres and regiments, the naval dockyards in Stockholm and Karlskrona, coastal artillery batteries in Stockholm, Blekinge, Gothenburg, and Gotland, and a number of air force bases".[70]

What is striking here is not merely the investigative assignment itself, which gave Lindencrona a timely opportunity to broaden and deepen his contacts within Sweden's military, but the Deference Shown to him by his hosts on these various visits. For example, the meticulous travel plan drawn up by the Defence Staff in Stockholm for his visit to the staff headquarters of the First Military District at Kristianstad – one of the seven military districts into which Sweden's military territory had been divided – even specified the exact time at which "director Lindencrona's car" should be sent in order to conduct him onwards to the air force's flight school F5 at Ljungbyhed in the southern county of Skåne.[71] Such is the special treatment normally accorded to a general – which, in a sense, is exactly what Lindencrona was.[72]

So how did Alvar Lindencrona come to be given such a senior appointment? "It was [Torsten] Nothin who chose him," claims former intelligence officer Ingemar Engman. The inference is entirely reasonable. Both government officials, Nothin and Lindencrona enjoyed a close relationship that likely began when Lindencrona was working in various government ministries.

"Nothin and Father were very good friends," recalls Elisabeth Lindencrona Paues and relates that Nothin was unique among her parents' acquaintances in being invited every year to stay in the family's summer house in Skanör, a seaside town in southern Sweden. Indeed, Elisabeth had to vacate her room for his visit.[73]

In his diary, Supreme Commander Helge Jung waspishly described Lindencrona as "Nothin's darling".[74] Two other entries by Jung – who understandably, given his position as head of Sweden's armed forces, appears to have taken umbrage at being sidelined in these discussions – confirm that Lindencrona was among those identified at the critical meeting with Prime Minister Tage Erlander "in the presence of [Jung's subordinate, Anders] Grafström" in June 1949 as being under consideration for a position in the planned resistance organization.[75]

We can also be certain that Nothin was authorized to make proposals about the resistance organization. For instance, he was effectively responsible for Carl August Ehrensvärd's appointment to the board as a military expert in 1949. According to Erlander's diary, Nothin justified his recommendation on the grounds that the Chief of the Army had "demonstrated, unlike many others during the war, a commitment to resistance" and, moreover, had "shown an interest in organizing an underground civilian defence".[76] Nothin may here have been remembering that it was Ehrensvärd who coined the "rousing slogan" that Prime Minister Per Albin Hansson announced to the public in 1943: "Any statement proclaiming the end of resistance will always be false."[77] In a popular book on modern warfare, Ehrensvärd had also underscored the importance, in the event of an attack on Sweden, of involving the "entire population in resistance". The book's title, which might be translated as *Fighting Fire with Fire*, also appears verbatim in Jung's diary as Supreme Commander as a working title for the resistance organization: "E-rd [Ehrensvärd] gave a briefing on several matters. […] The collaboration 'to fight fire with fire' works smoothly. Lindencrona brazen and self-assured; good. Grafström excellent."[78]

In light of all this, it might be thought that Torsten Nothin did not see himself as a suitable candidate for leader or even as a board member in the resistance organization. Quite apart from the fact that he was at this time partly physically incapacitated,[79] he had already assumed responsibility for the defence audit of 1949, which Nothin himself had felt should not address the issue of civil resistance. In order to avoid conflicting duties, Nothin was perhaps satisfied to have realized his long-standing plans for a resistance organization and secured as its director someone whom he trusted completely, namely Alvar Lindencrona.

## TELEGRAPH MAN

Torsten Nothin's deep interest in defence makes it likely that he was the person who nominated Håkan Sterky, an academic and civil servant, to become one of the sextuplets. Since the middle of the 1940s, Sterky had been a "key figure in Swedish defence research".[80] He played a leading role in the secret project to build a Swedish atom bomb by serving as chairman of the board of the Swedish National Defence Institute, which had been tasked with investigating possible military uses of atomic energy. He had also sat on the board of AB Atomenergi, a partly state-owned company that dealt with issues relating to uranium processing, and the government's coordinating body, the Atomic Committee.

Sterky's own research expertise lay in radio-and telecommunications, and as the director-general of the Swedish Telecommunications Authority (STA) he oversaw the expansion of these technologies in Sweden.[81] The STA had held a national monopoly on radio broadcasting since the end of the 1940s, which meant that Sterky had both experience of, and access to, technologies that were vital for the signals communications of a resistance organization, and for the transmission of information to the Swedish people. Sterky's formal responsibility for these areas on the board of the resistance organization is confirmed by Thede Palm's diary, in which Sterky is referred to as "Telegraph Man".

His duties included monitoring the purchase and testing of small radio transmitters for use by the resistance organization.

From this point on, it appears that Nothin's only contributions to the resistance organization were financial. "Nothin had called E-rd [Ehrensvärd] and asked if he needed money for a certain purpose," noted Helge Jung in his diary in January 1951, adding: "He could get plenty!!"[82] That Nothin's offer related to the resistance organization is confirmed by an entry in Erlander's diary dated April 1951 summarizing various topics that had been discussed during an hour-long meeting with Nothin: "Kempe had sent 100,000 crowns to Ehrensvärd to be used for Lindencrona's underground resistance organization. All very well, so long as Kempe doesn't imagine that he is supporting anything other than a purely defensive organization. Nothin had spoken to him about a secret intelligence service."[83]

"Kempe", who remains unidentified in the detailed list of individuals that accompanies the published edition of the diary, was most likely someone in the leadership troika of the forestry company Mo & Domsjö – either one of the brothers Erik and Ragnar Kempe or their cousin Carl Kempe, all of whom strongly supported initiatives for cultural preservation, and whose wealthy family, even today, continues to administer two public charities.[84] However, money was not the only thing that the industrial sector, in the broadest sense of the word, contributed to the resistance organization.

## IRON MAN

In the early 1990s, Bertil Jonsson, deputy chairman (and later chairman) of the Swedish Trade Union Confederation (LO), was personally briefed on the resistance organization by Curt-Steffan Giesecke, who was still in charge of its covert activities. "By that time I had already heard about it, from our end," recalls Jonsson, but adds that only a few people inside LO knew of the resistance organization's existence.[85] Based on Jonsson's own opinions, together with what he was told by others, the resistance organization grew out of the spirit of national unity and cooperation that LO and the Swedish Employers' Confederation (SAF) fostered in the post-war period. Indeed, public discussion of the resistance organization has more or less taken for granted that the two largest bodies in the Swedish labour market from the very beginning formed the resistance organization's core. However, now that we have identified the original sextuplets, a slightly different picture emerges. Although the resistance organization in its original form did give expression to a strong feeling of consensus, the parties involved were not capital and labour but workers and farmers.

Jonsson is right about LO's early involvement in the resistance organization: Arne Geijer, as we have seen, was the sixth member of its board. We can be very confident about this because a diary entry by Erlander from June 1954 locates Geijer in a meeting about how development of the resistance organization was progressing:

> Lindencrona, Geijer, Thede Palm, Major Grafström, director Stenqvist? [Elov Bergkvist] has given [Gunnar] Hedlund and me a summary of the preparations for a resistance organization in the event that Sweden should be partly or wholly occupied. As their summary makes clear, these preparations have been carried out in a highly effective manner and with every precaution.[86]

It is clear that Erlander is here referring to Arne Geijer, partly because of Geijer's own pocket calendar, and partly because of a note in Thede Palm's diary about the same meeting: "After a planning meeting yesterday at the home of Shaggy Man, Anders, Elov, and I made a presentation today at 11 o'clock to the Prime Minister, with the Minister of the Interior, Shaggy Man, and Iron Man in attendance."[87,88] As noted earlier, the codename "Shaggy Man" referred to Alvar Lindencrona, while "Iron Man" alluded playfully to Geijer's position as chairman of the Swedish Metalworkers' Union, known colloquially as Metall.

In all likelihood it was this position that made Geijer a person of interest for the resistance organization. With 231,000 members in critical manufacturing industries, Metall in the early 1950s was not only the largest but also the most prestigious body in the Trade Union Confederation. According to Geijer's biographer Charles Kassman, Swedish metalworkers were regarded as "the workers of the new era, truly men of the *machine age*, for whose area of expertise nothing seemed impossible".[89] By virtue of being their union leader, Geijer thus had a strong position within the labour movement, something he carefully exploited in order to raise his profile in public life:

> No other union leader, and few politicians apart from the party leaders, appeared in public debates as often as he did. When the press wanted opinions on union issues or more general political questions, newspapers turned as often to the chairman of Metall as they did to the head of LO itself.[90]

Geijer's authority and stature both within and outside union circles would probably have been a tremendous asset to the resistance organization if it had ever been forced to appear in the open. It is worth noting in this context that in the early 1950s Geijer was regarded as "so famous and popular" that the Social Democrats used his powerful masculine features in an election poster. As Kassman notes, "With its 'social realist' aura, the image could have been used as an illustration for the classic Swedish workers' song 'Arbetets söner' ('Sons of Labour')."[91] It was also probably of no small significance that during the great manufacturing strike of 1945 – "the fiercest but also the most important showdown between Social Democrats and their opponents on the far left since their parting of ways in 1917" – Geijer had come to grips with communists whose primary reason for striking was to divide Metall's membership for the purpose of social disruption.[92]

## COUNTRYMAN

It might seem like an obvious move to match Arne Geijer with Bertil Kugelberg – a labour leader and an employers' representative – on the board of the resistance organization. As was well known, the men were in close and frequent contact with each other. "They could have swapped jobs," explains Svante Nycander, the author of several books on Swedish labour history: "Geijer was rated as highly by employers as he was by members of LO, and the union liked Kugelberg. They had a similar perspective on the ethics of the labour market, were interested in what drove the other side, and agreed on almost everything."*[93]

The fact remains, however, that the honeymoon period of Swedish industrial relations and the inclusion of the Employers' Confederation in the resistance organization both lay in the future. The more natural partner for Geijer on the board in 1949–50 was a representative of the agricultural classes. The reason was the growing rapprochement between the Social Democrats and the Farmers' League since the early 1930s, which began with the so-called Crisis Agreement of 1933 that had been intended to tackle widespread unemployment and a collapse in the price of agricultural products.

This was its official purpose, at least; each party also had a deeper reason for collaborating. Per Albin Hansson later described the year of the Crisis Agreement as "a breakthrough year for the concept of consensus that makes democracy possible":

> The tensions between different social groups were easing. Farmers and workers began to understand that the contradiction between their respective interests was not so deep that it could not be resolved. […] Their common interests became clear as never before, and it felt like a release

* Svante Nycander passed away on 9 February 2024.

> from something warped when the people's representatives joined forces in a spirit of collaboration. It became possible to see a new kind of development, one in which the great mass of the people would together create a more secure society. We felt that democracy was by no means condemned to "endless bickering" but had at its disposal a capacity for decisive action that could and should be utilized.[94]

The Farmers' League expressed similar, albeit more nationalistically inclined, sentiments about the importance of "the national forces in all camps" coming together at a time of global tension.[95] For a brief period in the late 1930s, the Social Democrats and the Farmers' League had even formed a successful coalition government, and in 1951, after Tage Erlander established a personal relationship with the farmers' leader Gunnar Hedlund, they were again able to join in a coalition.[96]

By contrast, the famous "spirit of Saltsjöbaden" – a reference to the collective agreement of 1938 between the labour movement and employers – was not consolidated to any significant degree until after the ideologically fraught "Planned Economy" election of 1948. Erlander's first election since his surprising appointment as Prime Minister following the death of Per Albin Hansson, it represented the high point of the fierce struggles that took place over free enterprise in post-war Sweden. The new Social Democratic government, which lacked the forceful advocates of a planned economy whom Erlander had "inherited" from Hansson, managed to defuse tensions with the employers.[97] Even so, the moment can hardly have seemed propitious for a collaboration over something as sensitive as a secret resistance organization.

Since the Social Democrats had already established a relationship of trust with the Farmers' League, it could have been predicted that the original sextuplets would add to their number Anders E. Bjelle, whom Thede Palm variously refers to as "Farmer" and "Countryman" in his diary. It has been said that Bjelle was a man with a deep commitment to "combatting illness and distress", something that made him the Federation of Swedish Farmers' "self-appointed spokesperson on all such organizations and initiatives".[98]

However, I can also imagine another reason why Bjelle of all people should have become the farmers' representative in the resistance organization. Psychological warfare in both its offensive and defensive forms was at this time a fashionable concept in Sweden, and one of its earliest and more important promoters was Torsten Husén, a psychologist working for the Swedish military.[99] Manufacturing propaganda and other activities that come under the heading of psychological warfare were also something that the resistance organization engaged in. Thede Palm told the Neutrality Policy Commission that his operative level had responsibility for "communications" in the sense of "newspapers or ways of creating depots" of printed paper (a commodity that had been in short supply in occupied countries during World War II).[100] As Palm's diary makes clear, he and his group helped to write the newly added chapter on resistance spirit and resistance organizations in the 1961 edition of *If War Comes* – the state-produced preparedness brochure that was distributed to every home in Sweden during the Cold War and that must itself be considered a form of propaganda.[101]

In this light, it is worth noting that since the mid-1930s Bjelle had been managing director of the Federation of Swedish Farmers' publishing activities, which included a publishing house, a film department and a large number of successful periodicals. For example, its flagship organ *Jordbrukarnas Föreningsblad* reached a peak circulation of 378,000 in 1947.[102] Bjelle thus brought with him skills and an infrastructure of direct relevance for the waging of psychological warfare in various forms. When he died in June 1961, the spirit of collaboration in the labour market had become so established that employers had even "acquired a distinct liking for the Social Democratic labour movement".[103] By this point, the governmental collaboration between the Social Democrats and the Farmers' League – which changed its name to the Centre Party in 1958 – had been dissolved.

Replacing Bjelle on the resistance organization's board with a representative of the Employers' Confederation must have seemed not merely uncontroversial but almost expected.

## "CIVIL UNITY GOVERNMENT"

That Bertil Kugelberg is often mentioned in Thede Palm's diaries should not come as a surprise, because the Swedish Employers' Confederation often gave subsidies to T Bureau.[104] That support was specifically directed towards the intelligence service's economic research on Eastern Europe, a programme that was subsequently hived off as the East Economic Bureau.[105] But there is one entry on Kugelberg that warrants closer scrutiny. In December 1961, six months after Anders E. Bjelle's death, Palm wrote: "I was at Kugelberg's today where I had the opportunity among other things to invite him to the meeting on 9 January."[106] The entry for that date in January 1962 reads: "In the evening I made a long presentation at Alvar's place in which I went through everything I have been doing for the past year."[107] In turn, Alvar Lindencrona's pocket calendar contains a note on the same date: "poss[ibly] 6 at 7."[108]

The most reasonable explanation is that a meeting of the sextuplets had been scheduled for that evening for some time, and it was to this meeting that Palm was inviting Kugelberg as a new member. And, sure enough, Kugelberg noted in his diary that at 7pm he had a "Meeting at Lindencrona".[109] (Arne Geijer, his counterpart at the Trade Union Confederation, was probably absent because of a site visit on 9 January; judging from the deletion "Poss[ibly] Lindencrona" on the previous day in Geijer's diary, he had been expecting the sextuplets to meet then instead.[110]) Given Kugelberg's close involvement with the Swedish deep state, he must have known about the resistance organization's existence. As early as June 1949, Helge Jung wrote in his diary: "I regard Kugelberg as a good candidate [for the resistance organization's personnel]."[111] Kugelberg also knew Bjelle from the boards of the Swedish aid organizations

Norgehjälpen and Europahjälpen, which were active during and after World War II, respectively.[112]

But it seems to have been only now, on the cusp of the 1960s, that Kugelberg joined the sextuplets. Two other sources indicate that the Employers' Confederation's director then left the board as early as 1966, making him a member for considerably less time than has hitherto been assumed. The first source is a letter from Palm dated June 1966, written just prior to his departure as one of the resistance organization's operative heads, to Carl Eric Almgren, who was at that time Chief of the Defence Staff.[113] In it, Palm refers to "the new sextuplet", which suggests that a seat on the board had recently been vacated and that the board had elected a new member. The second source is Curt-Steffan Giesecke's own declaration to journalist Mikael Holmström that he "was taking part in meetings as far back as the 1960s".[114] Both pieces of information coincide with Kugelberg's retirement as director of the Employers' Confederation in late May 1966 and his succession by his "crown prince", Giesecke.[115]

Seen in this light, Bertil Kugelberg as an individual seems less relevant in the context of the "Men of 1949". A more interesting line of enquiry runs from the policies of mutual understanding between workers' and farmers' associations in the 1930s. It raises the question of why the resistance movement in its later phase of development instead oriented itself more explicitly towards the LO–SAF labour-employer axis.

---

From the start of the 1900s and, above all, after World War II, the Trade Union Confederation and the Employers' Confederation were given responsibility for the practical implementation of political decisions in a wide range of areas. Both organizations were for this reason included in the boards of government agencies and institutions. The two parties in the labour market, as political scientist Bo Rothstein explains, thereby became "*semi-official organs*, that is to say, neither parts of the state nor parts of civil society but rather some kind of chameleon-like hybrid".[116] Bertil Jonsson, who himself represented the Trade Union Confederation on the boards of several governmental bodies, describes the role of the two parties as follows: "They jointly brought politics into the real conditions of social life and the workplace. It was a strength in my view, but the Employers' Confederation pulled out [of the system] in the early 1990s."

Rothstein has given the name "corporative state" to this eminently Swedish form of public administration. A key function underlying its development was to create legitimacy for political reforms among the groups whom they directly affected and who were represented by one or other of the interest organizations, whose functionaries were appointed by the democratic order. A classic example is the formation in 1947 of the National Labour Market Board (AMS), which during the post-war period became the very "symbol of a uniquely Swedish labour market policy".[117] In the government bill, the responsible minister, Eije Mossberg, offered the following rationale for having a board comprising both parties in the labour market:

> Participation by representatives from the labour market bodies in not just the discussion phases but also in decision-making is also intended to create trust on the part of the individuals and thereby reinforce the board's authority. This is of special importance in light of the fact that many of the decisions which rest with the board should be assumed to be sensitive in nature and of far-reaching significance for large segments of the population.[118]

There is, in my view, an interesting and relevant connection to be made here to the resistance organization, which coincidentally would also fall under Mossberg's bailiwick.

In his historic study of resistance and resistance movements, Thede Palm states that the relationship to the "home front" is one of the most sensitive issues faced by every resistance organization, because the liberation struggle is dependent upon the support of ordinary people in the occupied country.[119] In which case, what could be more natural and fitting in post-war Sweden than to give each of the two giants of the labour market a prominent position in the organization? The legitimacy model of the "corporative state" offered a prototype for gaining the public's acceptance for continued resistance in occupied territory, particularly in a scenario in which the nation's political leadership has been eliminated.

A similar line of reasoning has been advanced by Göran Tunhammar, head of the Employers' Confederation and its successor, the Confederation of Swedish Enterprise: "When this was happening, the Trade Union Confederation and the Employers' Confederation were organizations that were regarded as essential to the functioning of society and collectively represented the majority of the population. They would have constituted a kind of civilian government of national unity."[120] Curt-Steffan Giesecke made a similar argument in his deposition to the Security Services Commission, which was appointed in 1999 to examine the activities of Sweden's security services since 1945. Regarding the involvement of the labour market's two main actors in the resistance organization, Giesecke stated that "it was important that such an organization have a broad base of support in society".[121] "In a country with a weaker social democracy and without Sweden's labour market corporatism," observes political scientist Björn von Sydow, "the resistance organization would perhaps have primarily operated via churches, shooting clubs, or other institutions whose members are active in formalized and nationwide structures, rather than via the Employers' Confederation and the trade unions."[122]

There is, in other words, a foundation of truth to the claims by media reports in the 1990s that the involvement of the labour market's two main parties was a strategy to establish a popular base for the Swedish resistance organization. It was, however, not in order to compensate for a lack of legality but because such an arrangement was typical of the country that the resistance organization was intended to defend. Might we even speak of a kind of interplay between the worker–employer cooperation in the labour market on the one hand, and cooperation within the resistance organization on the other – giving rise to mutual trust and a shared commitment to Sweden's continued development and security?

# 4

# The Operatives

## A PERFECT SPY

"His appearance was entirely grey: grey overcoat, grey cap, grey face. Yet beneath this dreary exterior there was clearly something important."[1] Thus Fredrik von Arnold, secretary to the Neutrality Policy Commission, recalls his first impression of Thede Palm when the former Swedish intelligence director was cross-examined by the Commission in February 1993. His sketch of Palm carries more than a whiff of George Smiley, the nondescript civil servant who is the hero – or antihero – of John le Carré's spy novels.

The connection is apt. In the few public photographs that exist of Palm, he bears an unmistakeable likeness to Alec Guinness's iconic portrayal of Smiley in the BBC's television adaptations of the 1970s and 1980s. Smiley's private musings in *Tinker Tailor Soldier Spy* (1974), the central text of le Carré's series, even suggest a similarity in the two men's characters: "At a certain moment, after all, every man chooses: will he go forward, will he go back? There was nothing dishonourable in not being blown about by every little modern wind. Better to have worth, to entrench, to be an oak of one's own generation."[2]

These lines echo what archivist Evabritta Wallberg remembers of Palm from their time together as colleagues at the Swedish

Military Academy, where he was posted after his departure from T Bureau: "Thede was out of step with the time we lived in. He was scrupulously formal, highly reserved, and in a world of his own."[3] Wallberg cites what she saw as a telling instance: that long after Swedes began to adopt less formal codes of speech, Palm continued to address her and other military wives by obsolete titles such as "madam colonel".

That a historian of religion who wrote a doctorate on Slavic cults and studied sacred groves should have been used for undercover operations further reinforces this impression that Palm would have been at home in the British secret service.[4] Ex-intelligence officer Jan Leijonhielm agrees: "It was the classic British way of doing things: so long as you had attended a top university, it didn't matter what you'd studied there. Even history of religion was acceptable."[5]

There were good reasons for having such a liberal hiring policy. In 1940, Palm, then working for Lund University's library, had volunteered for military service at C Bureau, the precursor to T Bureau. By that point Sweden's intelligence infrastructure had been neglected for many years. Clearly improvised, the newly formed unit was also short of staff.[6] Palm, who described himself ironically as a "cautious junior librarian from whom no one expected anything adventurous", was not the only unorthodox hire. On the contrary, as one journal article notes, "Librarians, archivists, and museum curators were a driving force in the formation of C Bureau."[7]

In his journal, Palm noted that his first posting for C Bureau was in Helsingborg, a city in southern Sweden close to occupied Denmark, where his mission was to "monitor border movements while posing as a passport official" and "remain generally alert".[8] His remit was to give advance notice of any German preparations for invading Sweden: "Had any sudden mobilization taken place in Denmark, I would unfailingly have learned of it." In the summer of 1941, he was assigned a similar investigative mission in a Norwegian-run refugee camp in Öreryd, a village in south-central Sweden, where he made a contact that would prove important. The camp's assistant director, Vilhelm Evang, went on to become Norway's director of intelligence after the war and played a key part in establishing the Norwegian stay-behind network.[9]

The intelligence work carried out by Palm and other so-called border representatives in the west and south of Sweden would be expanded by C Bureau's so-called group organizations (see Chapter 2), which included an embryonic resistance movement, the Homeland Stewardship entity. In 1943, Palm was put in charge of P Group, which operated along the border between the central Swedish counties of Värmland and Dalarna. Its methods would establish a template for all of the group organizations.[10]

---

With the storm clouds of war dispersing, the activities of C Bureau ceased to be politically viable. In January 1946, Minister of Defence Allan Vougt observed to Carl August Ehrensvärd, his Chief of the Defence Staff, that "things might come up" about Sweden's cooperation with other national intelligence services that could be damaging for its official policy of neutrality.[11] As a precautionary measure, Vougt recommended the firing of C Bureau's director, Major Carl Petersén.

Ehrensvärd agreed but argued that Petersén had played far too public a role for him to be able to serve as head of the secret intelligence service, someone whose identity "should be unknown to most people".[12] From this perspective, the unobtrusive Thede Palm was an ideal successor to Petersén. His eldest daughter, Ebba Palm-Lamoureux, recalls that her father never discussed his work and allowed her to tell school friends only that he was a historian: "Nothing else whatsoever!"[13]

How exactly this putative historian filled his days received not a single mention in the Swedish press during the entire time that Palm served as Sweden's director of intelligence.[14] Only in

1965, when he moved to the Swedish Military Academy and began writing articles on military history for a Stockholm daily, did Palm become what Evabritta Wallberg calls "acknowledged" – someone able to enjoy and take pride in an official existence. Indeed, being openly employed with a "job title and suchlike, and nothing to do with secrecy" was the main motivation behind Palm's request to be posted to the Academy.[15]

Yet so long as Palm remained bound by conditions of secrecy, he was careful to avoid drawing attention to himself. For example, he once took his young daughter Ebba to the zoo as a cover for a meeting he had arranged with Vilhelm Evang. "The reason I never forgot that day was that at one point I mistakenly took the other man's hand instead of my father's," recalls Ebba Palm-Lamoureux. "They were both identically dressed and I reached for the wrong trench coat."

Palm's correspondence does nonetheless contain a rare moment of self-revelation, when the Royal Dramatic Theatre in Stockholm considered staging a play in summer 1950 with his name as author. The theatre's literary advisor, poet Hjalmar Gullberg, was firm in his report on the play and noted of its title, *Knowing Yourself*: "It is the Ibsenesque viewpoint… Knowing yourself means revealing yourself."[16] Even at this early phase of his leadership of Sweden's intelligence service, Palm clearly longed to appear in his own name – to gain recognition and acceptance as someone to be reckoned with.

The new intelligence service that Palm was hired to create would be small but effective.[17] For example, T Bureau's network of Baltic agents during the 1940s and 1950s was able to establish the location of almost all Soviet airbases. The KGB, notes historian Michael Fredholm, "rated Palm's organization […] far more highly than later Swedish commentators have credited".[18] But it was not only as an adversary that Palm commanded respect. His status is also attested to in the long and cordial correspondence between Allen Dulles, legendary director of the CIA, Nicholas Elliott, the MI6 intelligence officer who extracted a confession from double-agent Kim Philby, and Reinhard Gehlen, head of West Germany's intelligence service.[19] According to the British, Palm was "one of the least tractable individuals [we] have ever dealt with".[20]

Similar insights are offered by William Colby, whose memoir *Honorable Men: My Life in the CIA* portrays Palm as:

> A quiet, intellectual, self-effacing gentleman of the old school [...] the prototype of the silent spymaster, his head full of exotic secret adventures, while he maintained the image of a nondescript and not particularly exceptional middle-grade civil servant.[21]

Another incident that confirms his status among the Western powers took place in summer 1963. Following an exchange with Jack Kaufman, the CIA's station chief in Stockholm, Palm wrote in his diary that although the highly public exposure of Stig Wennerström, an air force colonel who had passed secrets to the Soviets, was unquestionably a "serious setback" for relations between Swedish Defence Staff and the West, his own contact network was unlikely to be affected. On the contrary, he might "serve as a bridge in the near future".[22]

The previous year Palm had nonetheless been greatly embarrassed by the CIA.[23] On 22 October 1962, Palm returned to T Bureau following an extended stay in Washington, DC, where he had met with the CIA's new leadership. In a letter to Deputy Director for Plans Richard "Dick" Helms dated the same day, Palm shared his conviction that Swedish contacts with the American intelligence service remained strong.[24] T Bureau had for some time helped to "keep the Baltic region under control" in exchange for material from the CIA relating to "trouble spots and suchlike that might become flashpoints for a full-scale war".[25] That same day, President John F. Kennedy announced in a television address that the Soviet Union was in the process of deploying medium-range nuclear missiles in Fidel Castro's Cuba. "It very nearly broke me," Palm later confessed to Kaufman.[26]

Just days earlier, Palm had visited the CIA in Washington, where he had discussed Cuba but evidently not been informed about the looming crisis. His position in Stockholm could have become "quite impossible" had his ignorance of the nuclear missiles become known. His only stroke of luck was that he did not get the chance to submit a report on the visit to his superiors until after the news had broken. In this way Palm was able to "give the impression of being more informed" than was actually the case.[27]

This ostracism, so uncharacteristic of relations between the CIA and T Bureau, continued throughout the crisis. As Palm afterwards complained: "Not until the middle of the second week [of the crisis] did we get a phone call regarding the situation in Cuba and [the CIA's] assessment of the global situation."[28] Even so, his own organization, which was keeping the Baltic under control, managed to form their own – solid and somewhat surprising – picture of the crisis as it developed. In relation to 23 October, the second day of the crisis, Palm later noted in his diary that the situation was "considerably calmer than at the same time last year" and added: "Russian movement in the Baltic area and in the Eastern bloc entirely failed to materialize."[29]

On 24 October, an American naval blockade of Cuba came into force, and the day after T Bureau observed the return of a Russian vessel that had left the Baltic three days earlier. "It had been bound for Cuba," Palm wrote in his diary, "and must therefore have received orders on the 23rd to turn back, which means that the Russians had by that point already decided to act with caution."[30]

On the basis of this and previous information, Palm was able to reassure a "deeply shaken" Israeli intelligence officer that he regarded the situation "since this morning [of the 25th] as much calmer".[31] Yet it had only slowly become clear to Washington's decision-makers that the situation was stabilizing. In Florida, an invasion force had gathered whose size recalled the massing of Allied forces in southern England prior to D-Day.[32]

Why was Palm kept out of the loop? Jack Kaufman, the CIA's representative in Stockholm, would later claim that the real reason was "the extraordinarily strict orders [for secrecy] issued by the White House".[33] While Kaufman's rationale is plausible enough, we can also speculate about another possibility. If the Soviet Union's deployment of offensive nuclear missiles in Cuba was the first step towards a full-scale war – rather than a more symbolic gesture in support of Third World communist states, as modern historians with access to Moscow archives argue – an American ground invasion would look like a justified and necessary reaction.[34] For months prior to the missile crisis, the CIA under Richard Helms had been planning a new attack on Cuba (including against Castro himself) in response to the Bay of Pigs invasion debacle of 1961. Indeed, initiatives of this kind would continue to be taken even *during* the Cuban Missile Crisis. The CIA could thus have had only limited interest in Swedish intelligence that there were no signs of Soviet mobilization in the Baltic area.[35]

As late as 6 November 1962, by which point most of the Soviet missiles were being dismantled, Kaufman could declare that "the Cuban crisis was continuing and remained as serious as before", a statement that Palm "flatly denied".[36]

---

It would be a "difficult day" for Thede Palm on 27 December 1964.[37] After 19 years as head of T Bureau, he found himself being thanked by its staff members and thrust out into the cold. Palm had been thinking about the "issue of the firm's crown prince" for over a decade.[38] For some time, he had been looking forward to tendering his resignation near the decade's end; he had even discussed the matter with his presumptive successor, Birger

Elmér, head of domestic intelligence at the so-called B Bureau.[39] But in November he had received a summons from Minister of Defence Sven Andersson, who informed him that T Bureau and B Bureau would shortly be merged into a new entity and that he was not being considered for the role of director.[40] That position went instead to Birger Elmér, who as early as the following year would be heading a new, integrated intelligence service whose name and activities, particularly overseas, would be exposed in a humiliating and ignominious fashion during the so-called "IB Affair" of 1973.

Elmér "took it like a gentleman and a good sport", recalls journalist Jan Guillou, whose exposé made the IB director a "highly recognizable" figure but eventually also a good friend of his.[41] "We were like two wartime officers who met up again after the cessation of hostilities," recalls Guillou, who even secured Elmér's help in creating the intrigues that inform his famous spy novel series about Swedish intelligence officer Carl Hamilton.

Replacing Palm with Elmér was "in many regards a poor decision", observes Jan Leijonhielm: "No investigation has ever properly established how it came about." Over the years, Palm's dismissal has attracted many explanations, ranging from personal vendettas to the need to repair the damage caused by Stig Wennerström's treason.[42] The present study offers a more comprehensive explanation that also considers other reasons: that by the mid-1960s, the aura of anachronism surrounding Palm had become a liability. Elmér – a self-confessed socialist in a black polo-neck sweater who abandoned a career in psychoanalysis and was, according to his mentee and colleague Ingemar Engman, "pals with everyone" – embodied the new spirit of the times, presenting a stark contrast to Palm's reserved and conservative manner.[43] Moreover, as Jan Guillou gleefully reveals, Elmér was a "frivolous" person, someone who echoed the new liberal attitude towards personal relationships by "shamelessly detailing his sexual exploits". Evabritta Wallberg takes a similar view: "The transition from Palm to Elmér paralleled in microcosm the way that Sweden was changing and being revolutionized." Her remarks echo the declaration made by le Carré's traitor in *Tinker Tailor Soldier Spy* that secret services are "the only real measure of a nation's political health, the only real expression of its subconscious".[44]

---

Shortly after leaving T Bureau, Thede Palm ended his involvement with the secret resistance movement too. He had joined in autumn 1949, when Anders Grafström sounded Palm out about becoming "number two in G's special remit" in a personal capacity rather than as a representative of the intelligence service.[45] Prior to that point, Grafström had been the only staff officer at the operational level who answered to the then five-member board.

Palm was doubtful about the whole enterprise because it lacked a budget. "Less than 250,000 crowns a year is not going to do it," he cautioned Grafström.[46] Palm's impression was not improved when he met the governing board at a meeting which he had been invited to address on the topic of – *nota bene* – "homeland stewardship":

> It was a rather odd gathering. The questions asked of me were surprisingly simple, and I was unable to form any conception of how my lecture had been received. When it was over, the chairman [Eije Mossberg] invited me to step outside for a moment, and after about ten minutes he joined me and asked me to what extent I was interested in joining them as a colleague. The whole business was highly formal and utterly ridiculous. We then returned to the assembled and announced in joyful tones that I had unhesitatingly accepted the commission. I have since heard that everyone was lyrical about my lecture and extremely interested. However, I left there at half past midnight, none the wiser about the nature of the association I had just joined, and went home to bed and to nurse a cold.[47]

Despite, or perhaps because of his initial scepticism, Palm became one of the most active and influential figures in the first generation of the resistance movement. By the time he left in summer 1966, he had assumed operative responsibility for intelligence issues in general, and signals and communications in particular, as well as the management of "internal security".[48] The latter, as Palm subsequently explained in his history of resistance movements, involves defending against "enemy surveillance and infiltration", inter alia by monitoring the members of the resistance group and clamping down on "careless talk".[49]

After being edged out of the Defence Staff, Palm wrote to Alvar Lindencrona that "cooperation on our front ought to be able to continue".[50] Some months later, in June 1965, Chief of the Defence Staff Carl Eric Almgren personally invited Palm to remain involved in "special operations" on the grounds that Almgren "'had been forced' to put two eggs [i.e. T Bureau and B Bureau] in the same basket" and was not keen to "include a third one [i.e. the resistance movement]".[51] In Almgren's opinion, having one person, Birger Elmér, in charge of both domestic and foreign intelligence was already "a bit much".[52] Yet just one year later, Palm also resigned his underground responsibilities, telling the Neutrality Policy Commission that he had been "fired for a second time" and that Lindencrona was behind it.[53]

Although the claim may sound strange, Palm and Lindencrona had never seen eye to eye during their involvement with the resistance movement. This was partly a clash of personalities: Lindencrona was sociable and extroverted, qualities that irritated Palm. Under cross-examination by the Neutrality Policy Commission, Palm even questioned whether Lindencrona had been the right person to lead the resistance movement in view of the fact that he was "so extraordinarily open" and "willing to talk about things".[54]

Palm's diary entries from this period contain several examples of what he had in mind. At one meeting, he claimed, Lindencrona had unexpectedly declared that "he had engaged a new gentleman […] whom he had apparently briefed fully on the whole matter" – a point of information that left those present "somewhat aghast".[55] On another occasion, Palm learned that Lindencrona was planning to go to Paris "with special instructions, as he had done before" – presumably on a secret mission from Prime Minister Tage Erlander to bolster efforts to secure French support for Sweden becoming affiliated with the European Common Market. "It had nothing to do with me," wrote Palm, "but he [Lindencrona] was nonetheless talking about it."[56]

There was, however, a deeper reason for their falling out, which we will examine in greater detail in the following chapter, namely the resistance movement's relationship to the Western powers. In a published autobiographical sketch, Palm notes that he was from early on "insistent upon the fact that whatever we organized should be under the command of Swedes".[57] In his view, independence was not an obstacle to the resistance movement collaborating with the British and the Americans. Yet the scale and depth of those ties, like the question of who should manage them, was a bone of contention between him and Lindencrona from the very start. According to Palm's diary entry from this period, Lindencrona in April 1965 proposed finding an opportunity when he might "contact the CIA's new director and explain Sweden's position [with regard to the US]".[58] Palm merely replied that it was something that should be given further thought. Nonetheless, Palm was to record in his memoir that Lindencrona went ahead and on his own initiative made a visit without informing Palm.

This action seems to have triggered a definitive rupture between the two men, possibly because Lindencrona had already, to Palm's great irritation, "played at being ambassador on his own initiative" with the CIA's previous director, Walter Bedell Smith.[59] Even so, it is doubtful that Palm, as he later recalled in the early 1990s, left the resistance movement because he was dismissed from his post. The more likely explanation is that he resigned because he had had enough. Even before

Palm was forced out of T Bureau, he had contemplated leaving the resistance movement because of its internal tensions and the waning support in certain quarters of the government for both the project itself and his own personal involvement. As he observed in June 1964, "this will likely be my last year".[60] By this point, he was not alone among the operatives of the resistance movement in feeling dissatisfied.

## THE UNHAPPY ONE

It will be remembered that the trio who formed the staff of the resistance organization also included Anders Grafström and an individual who was still alive when Thede Palm testified to the Neutrality Policy Commission and whom Palm therefore refused to identify. In the hearings, Elov Bergkvist, a graduate in business administration and a life-long insurance man, was only ever alluded to cryptically as an "unhappy" person.[61] However, his identity is betrayed by Palm's recurrent references in his diary of these years to working meetings about the resistance organization with "Elov and Anders", and by the fact that someone with that unusual first name worked for many years as director of finance and sales at Thule under Alvar Lindencrona.[62] Like Palm, Bergkvist sent a signed letter to Chief of the Defence Staff Carl Eric Almgren in summer 1966 in which he stated his "decision to leave the organization".[63]

According to Palm, it was Bergkvist who had operative responsibility for psychological warfare within the resistance organization. Bergkvist seems to have carried out these activities in some kind of collaboration with the Psychological Defence Board, a government agency that had been formed on the initiative of Eije Mossberg.[64] It is possible that the resistance organization functioned as a kind of precursor and pioneer for the board's wartime organization, the State Information Agency, which had been tasked with finding ways to "protect [...] the normal organs of information: newspapers, magazines, radio, etc." and facilitate the free circulation of news and opinion.[65]

A resistance organization might, for example, collect factual material on news relating to the home front or assist in the production and distribution of illegal publications that advocate resistance in a broad sense.[66]

What is undeniably clear is that the board's director, political scientist Gunnar Heckscher, took an interest in the resistance organization's activities and was also kept informed about them.[67,68] There were also direct personal connections between the two organizations. During the 1950s and early 1960s, Curt-Steffan Giesecke would, in the event of war, have been appointed head of the division within the State Information Agency that had responsibility for areas such as the media's technological preparedness, telecommunications and the disruption of foreign radio broadcasts to Sweden.[69]

The main reason why Elov Bergkvist grew increasingly "unhappy" with his role within the resistance organization, to the point that he repeatedly requested to be relieved of his duties, seems to have been a long-standing personal conflict with Alvar Lindencrona. When, in 1954, Bergkvist was appointed head of Fylgia, a rival insurance company, he told Palm how happy he was to "get away from Shaggy Man", who, Bergkvist claimed, "was unable to keep quiet" about his role in the resistance organization among employees at Thule.[70] Shortly thereafter, the animosity between the two men boiled over. On one occasion, Palm records in his diary, Bergkvist received a visit from an "absolutely furious" Lindencrona, who wanted to "provoke a complete rupture", presumably because the latter regarded Bergkvist as imprudently having established contacts with the government of a kind that were more appropriate to the head of the resistance organization.[71]

## THE HERO OF MÄRKÄJÄRVI

Anders Grafström seems to have taken his fights with Alvar Lindencrona with greater equanimity. Because of Thule's investment in a rescue organization in the early 1960s, whose advantages Lindencrona fatally overestimated, Grafström wrote tartly in a letter to Carl August Ehrensvärd that "'Shaggy Man' wasn't such a superman from our perspective either".[72] But Grafström had fewer dealings with Lindencrona than either Elov Bergkvist or Thede Palm. Within the resistance organization he was mainly concerned with what Palm called "weapons issues" and, beyond that, recruitment and training of the regional organization below the operative level.[73]

A draft autobiography that Grafström left incomplete upon his death in October 1979 states that he went "directly from the school bench" to officer training at the cavalry school in Skövde and then to the Military Academy at Karlberg.[74] And only days after he received his commission at the Norrland Dragoon Regiment in Umeå, he found himself in the thick of things. "Disturbances were reported from Ådalen," explains Grafström in his draft:

> The radio and the newspapers accounted for the protracted and intense labour conflict at the sulphate factories in Marmarverken and Sandviken as well as the sulphite factory in Utansjö. The employer had called in strike-breakers to load the wood pulp. They had been billeted in barracks at Lunde, just south of Kramfors. On the first day when the strike-breakers appeared, there were violent protests. The demonstrators managed to enter the factory premises in Sandviken by simply lifting the gate off its hinges. They also got onto the quay where the work was in progress. Violent confrontations took place and some of the strike-breakers were very roughly handled and forced to accompany a procession of demonstrators to Kramfors.[75]

Because of the violence, soldiers – eventually including Grafström – were sent to the area. The events which then unfolded propelled the Social Democrats into an unbroken period of government lasting four decades and, at least in popular opinion, led to the passage of an outright ban, which remains in force, against the deployment of soldiers in domestic conflicts during peacetime. The soldiers at Ådalen opened fire, killing five demonstrators.

Grafström's account of the Ådalen disaster nonetheless differs significantly from the version that was subsequently presented by the modern Swedish labour movement and director Bo Widerberg's international prize-winning film *Ådalen 31* (1969).[76] Putting the shootings in a context of chaos and widespread lawlessness, Grafström argues that the authorities had unreasonable expectations of what a military intervention would mean. According to Grafström, when soldiers first arrived in the *Ådalen* area on 13 May, they were met by shouts of "point your weapons the 'right way'", i.e. towards the strike-breakers. At the barracks, he notes, "further rioting took place with stone-throwing and threats to both officers and soldiers" at the same time as the electricity supply to the camp was sabotaged. "Orders were issued to launch smoke grenades along with two volleys of blank rounds", at which the demonstrators "merely laughed". Standing beside the striking workers in the crowd were communists loyal to the Soviet Union, who called to the soldiers: "Russia will come and help us."[77]

Shortly before leaving the regimental base in Umeå on 14 May, Grafström learned that live shots had been fired in Ådalen earlier in the day. He recalled "feeling the gravity of the moment". During the journey south, the soldiers' train carriages were pelted with stones and buckshot by what he calls "civilian patrols" lying in ambush along the railway line. Obstacles deliberately placed on the track also threatened to derail the train. Upon arriving, Grafström's men were "abused and spat on", but there was no further violence. The government quickly ordered the military to leave Ådalen.[78]

Grafström's memoirs also contain a description of how the soldiers discussed these events on their way home:

> No one was in any doubt as to the fact that an appalling tragedy had taken place [...] at the cost of innocent people's lives.

> But whose fault was it? Was it our fault that the government ordered us to assist in restoring order? The county governor who requisitioned soldiers and the government who ordered their deployment knew that conscripts are neither trained nor equipped for maintaining law and order. We are armed for war.[79]

On this occasion it was Grafström who faced a weaker opponent. But in much of his subsequent career as a soldier, it was he, figuratively speaking, who would be lifting his hand against a more powerful adversary.

---

A decade after events in Ådalen, in the winter of 1939/40, Finland was attacked by the Soviet Union. A wave of Nordic enthusiasm swept across Sweden. Many Swedes, writes historian Göran Andolf, "were inspired by sympathy with their sister country and by a feeling of kinship with Finland that had its roots in what they felt was their shared history and culture".[80] "Finland's cause is ours" became a popular slogan but not for idealistic reasons alone: Soviet planes and ships based along the Gulf of Bothnia, only minutes of flying time from Stockholm, would have drastically restricted Sweden's room for manoeuvre.

With Carl August Ehrensvärd, at this point a lieutenant colonel, as its prime mover, and the Trade Union Confederation and the Employers' Confederation present in the background as economic and legitimizing forces, a Swedish contingent of almost 9,000 volunteers was dispatched to Finland's Winter War. One of them was Anders Grafström, whose mission would be to lead a "ranger unit trained in reconnaissance and sabotage" in Finnish Lappland.[81] In March 1940, his company fought in the first major action between Swedish volunteers and Soviet forces, the outcome of which was tersely summarized in the newspaper headline "Two Hundred Russians Fall to Swedish Bullets".[82] Fighting behind enemy lines for five hours, 90 Swedes fought 400 Soviets, killing almost half. Swedish casualties numbered only six dead and seven injured. In reference to the battle's location, Grafström would henceforth be called the "hero of Märkäjärvi".[83]

Grafström's commandos also served in the Continuation War that began in June 1941. The support of Swedish volunteers for Finland was more controversial this time because Finnish and German forces were fighting together against the Soviet Union under the so-called Anti-Comintern Pact. The ranks of the volunteers also included around a hundred organized Nazis.[84] Unlike the Winter War, Swedes who travelled to Finland in 1941 were not given permission to use Swedish materiel but had instead to make do with improvised weaponry and what Grafström remembered as "very peculiar outfits": "When my company marched to Åbo station for transportation to the front, forty or so of the men were wearing dress shirts and silk socks."[85]

The main achievement of this motley crew was to recover the strategic naval base in the port town of Hangö in the Gulf of Finland, which had been lost to the Soviet Union under the humiliating terms of the Moscow Peace Treaty of 1940. Grafström's Third Company marched towards the town by the light of the moon and in freezing cold, in constant danger from booby traps. Upon arrival, the men found the town abandoned. Grafström raised a Finnish naval flag in the main square in front of the city hall, which the temporary Soviet administration had renamed First of May Square 12, and the company shouted a resounding "God Save Finland!"[86]

For the rest of the war, Grafström worked at the Defence Staff headquarters in Stockholm, including with Sweden's armed support for the Danish resistance. This experience, together with his service in Finland, almost certainly played a key part in sparking his interest in how to wage a resistance campaign against an occupying power. By 1944 he had already begun to give lectures on "partisan warfare" in civil defence circles.[87] When the end of hostilities in Europe quickly gave way to fears about another war, Anders Grafström was well suited to spearhead the contingency planning for a Swedish defeat.

# PART THREE

# Well-Organized Defeat

# 5

# Operation Metro

### "A PURELY SWEDISH ORGANIZATION"

It is a truth universally acknowledged that every new organization is in need of a name. In the case of the Swedish resistance organization, finding a name seems to have been a difficult process. A number of suggestions were considered – one "completely crazy", according to Thede Palm – before an agreement was reached in the last days of 1950.[1] Until now, it has been assumed that the new name was Stay behind. But neither Alvar Lindencrona's daughter Elisabeth nor his son Gustaf recalls their father ever using that term to refer to the resistance organization.

Hans Wermdalen was director of the Swedish security service's A Bureau for several years in the early 1970s, overseeing the monitoring of Soviet radio communications with Russian sleeper cells in Sweden, and had responsibility within the resistance organization for "securing its communications behind enemy lines". He, too, has no memory of "Stay behind" being used as a name: "I imagine it rather as a description of the organization's activities."[2] Curt-Steffan Giesecke, who succeeded Lindencrona as commander, seems to have made a similar point when explaining the organization's purpose: "To *stay behind*, sustain the resistance, and cause damage to the occupying power."[3] The term thus seems to be an adjective, as in *stay-behind organization*, rather than a name. In the title of this book, *Stay Behinds* serves quite happily as a noun.

This conclusion is supported by the fact that "Stay behind" was not used as a name within the Norwegian organization as well as by the scholarship on special forces and paramilitary groups.[4] Indeed, there are references to "stay-behind groups" in the survey of different forms of resistance that was jointly published by the Swedish Defence University in Stockholm and the US Special Operations Command Europe in 2019.[5] It is even possible to distinguish between categories of stay-behind groups. A clearly military category is the reconnaissance patrols dispatched by a retreating army that then stay on inside enemy-occupied territory and certain types of special forces units. Other categories include civilian resistance networks established during peacetime.[6]

Parallel stay-behind structures like these have existed in Sweden. Documents that I have inspected but will refrain from citing here indicate that as late as the 1990s Swedish commando units were being trained to perform certain resistance organization-like tasks within occupied territory. These activities have their origins in World War II, when carefully selected military personnel were directed to lead members of fragmented units on small-scale campaigns of irregular warfare, what has been called *free war*.[7] There are other comparable examples, too. The intelligence service T Bureau and its successor IB had war organizations involving volunteers and conscripts, both of whom were to "stay behind where they lived" in the event of war and carry out intelligence-gathering activities.[8]

So what name should we use to designate the civilian stay-behind group that existed in Sweden during the Cold War? Two phrases that recur frequently in Thede Palm's diaries are "homeland stewardship" and the less appealing "industrial protection", which may be a reference to the private sector's support for the resistance organization or, alternatively, a term borrowed from personnel vetting programmes in Swedish industry. However, both should be seen as descriptive terms, which may have been used only by Palm. Since a name was needed, why not a name that worked internationally? In neighbouring Norway, those responsible for the equivalent stay-behind group had reasoned that its three bases – the intelligence network "Lindus", the sabotage division "Rocambole" and the extraction entity "Blue Mix" – could hardly be named after famous Norwegian skiers "if we are to make ourselves understood abroad".[9] According to Palm's diary, the Swedes ultimately opted for "Operation Metro", a name that carries suitable connotations of subways and other underground structures.[10]

---

The codename was decided at the same time as the board members were wrestling with the fundamental issue of the resistance organization's "relationship to foreign powers" – in this case not Eastern powers but Western.[11] This was a ticklish problem to solve, and not only for the Swedes. Documents issued by NATO headquarters and the CIA in the early 1950s announced grandly that allies and sympathetic neutral countries should create stay-behind groups, under strictly national control, as part of their defences against global communism.[12] The reality was more complicated. As Norwegian historians Olav Riste and Arnfinn Moland observe: "Within the alliance, tensions between national control and NATO oversight were to be a recurrent theme in negotiations over the [operative] coordination of the secret services."[13] Such tensions arose whether the negotiations related to stay-behind groups or to conventional intelligence activities.

Norway's head of intelligence, Vilhelm Evang, who, admittedly, had accepted financial support from Western powers for his country's stay-behind organization, felt it necessary on several occasions to draw attention to the issue of national ownership. As late as the mid-1960s, he remained dissatisfied with the degree of American influence, his colleague Thede Palm recalls.[14] Palm himself had long been concerned that foreign powers might have too much say over Sweden's resistance organization. In autumn 1949, while Palm was discussing "the whole question of homeland stewardship" with Harry Carr, British intelligence agency MI6's Controller Northern Area, the latter promptly offered him special training in "certain types of [radio] transmissions".[15] Presumably these related to frequencies and codes intended for use during an occupation of Sweden: 12 months earlier Carr had suggested that this might be something on which MI6 and a Swedish resistance organization under the direction of T Bureau might collaborate with a view to avoiding an "[unpredictable] 1939-style scenario".[16] Although Palm saw clearly that collaboration in several areas might be necessary, he observed somewhat sceptically that "if we have to deal with Harry's people, we will to some degree have to adapt ourselves to their terms".[17]

As quickly became apparent, this – and more – was exactly what Britain and the United States had in mind. According to Palm, in January 1951 both countries' intelligence services announced that they wished "to place the entire operation under their control".[18] For the Swedes, it was an unacceptable proposal. The resistance organization had already decided as a matter of principle to remain "a purely Swedish organization with only lines of communication to the West". Contact with the Western powers would not be an end in itself but "a relatively insignificant means".[19] Army Chief Carl August Ehrensvärd regarded involvement with the West as both defeatist and politically explosive, and he questioned whether a resistance organization in non-aligned Sweden "should have anything at all to do with the Americans".[20]

Relations with the West thus needed to be clarified and delimited. Palm, now authorized to speak for the resistance organization and "make final decisions", was sent to London to establish the ground rules for collaboration with the British and Americans. Marcus Wallenberg had given him a piece of advice about negotiation technique: to avoid the risk of being forced into a bad compromise, "never decide beforehand that you will bring back a result".[21] The advice of the experienced businessman proved valuable, according to the account in Palm's diary:

> Monday the 22nd [of January] was the hardest day, and it made me recall MW's advice. [...] The other side made concessions on every point, and the unquestioned result is precisely what I wanted, namely that Metro is to be a fully Swedish organization under Swedish control that can benefit from help and advice from the West, but nothing more.[22]

Chief of the Defence Staff Carl Eric Almgren and Curt-Steffan Giesecke both confirmed that this arrangement would be implemented. As Almgren told the Neutrality Policy Commission in 1993, "We took the line that that there would be no question of doing something at the behest of the Americans [...] and so it was in the years that followed."[23]

Giesecke told journalist Mikael Holmström that "this [resistance] organization was not created for the purposes of collaborating with the United States" and that during his own time as commander he had "no contact with Americans, let alone the CIA" and worked with the British only in the acquisition of radio technology and making test broadcasts to British receivers.[24] As Hans Wermdalen, former bureau chief of the security service, remarks: "We would drive the enemy from our territory but were more or less alone. We and Finland were part of a network of Nordic stay-behind organizations but, as far as I am aware, had no collaboration with [the Anglo-American] NATO." These accounts all give the lie to the notion that the Swedish resistance organization was more or less under NATO command, a perspective that has been largely shaped by the memoirs of CIA officer William Colby – what authors Daniele Ganser and Mats Deland claim is "an important source".[25]

In the chapter dealing with his time in Stockholm in the early 1950s, Colby claims that his role in the American intelligence service was to "plan and implement [...] stay-behind networks in Scandinavia". This involved "deciding which assignments they should take, what kinds of provisions and how many people they needed, and how they should organize themselves". According to Colby, in neutral territories whose governments had adopted policies that precluded collaboration with NATO, the CIA "would need to do the job itself or, in the best case scenario, with 'unofficial' help from local agencies".[26]

The copy of his memoirs that I borrowed from the Swedish Defence University contains a handwritten note, taped to the inside of the folder, that comments on the trustworthiness of Colby's account: "Thede – I didn't think you [would want] this autographed, so it's not. Nor can I say I hope you enjoy it. Well, anyway, here it is." The note is signed simply "Edward" and addressed to Thede Palm, who evidently had the book sent to him. The sender – probably Edward Ryan, another CIA officer who was active in Stockholm in the 1950s – seems to have assumed that Palm would not appreciate its contents. If so, there were good reasons. Palm's diaries for this period make no mention of William Colby in the key role that the American claims for himself in his memoirs. Nor do they anywhere refer to advanced preparations for an American-led stay-behind organization on Swedish soil.

What do Palm's diaries say instead? In May 1951, Palm was asked to meet Colby "about a special matter":

> I hesitated. *I have nothing whatever to do with him.* [...] An American acting on behalf of the embassy but not belonging to the embassy has left a radio transmitter beneath the floor of a barn belonging to the artist Arvid Knöppel in Gunnarskog. Knöppel knew nothing about it. The transmitter is to be used only in the event of a foreign occupation of Sweden. Knöppel discovered the transmitter while rebuilding his barn and has likely handed it over to the police. Colby is now wondering what to do. On Wednesday I contacted [head of the security service Åke] Hasselrot and put the entire matter in his hands, asking him to sort it out.[27]

In sum, Colby gives the impression of being an amateur, someone given to embellishing the truth whose activities threatened to disrupt or, in the worst case, expose Sweden's Metro organization. In this he was not alone.

## "EVERYONE IS FURIOUS"

Approximately a year later, in March 1952, Thede Palm was approached by Ragnar Liljeblad, an engineer and now a retired manager of the electrical company Asea. According to Palm's diary, Liljeblad explained that "he and some other industrialists were involved in industrial protection" and asked Palm for "help with major preparations for what would essentially be a mass evacuation [of the civilian population]".[28] Palm was very unhappy about Liljeblad contacting him, an introduction that was evidently made by the Chief of the Defence Staff Richard Åkerman. Palm was quite unwilling to start discussing the subject of "industrial protection", or organized resistance, with a complete stranger. Moreover, as Palm later recalled, the man gave a "quite confused impression".[29]

Presumably in order both to avoid further dealings with Liljeblad and to investigate a possible competing resistance organization initiative, Palm promised to put him in touch with Anders Grafström, "who understood the kind of matters" that their conversation touched on. This would be the beginning of a criminal investigation of a member of Ragnar Liljeblad's circle that ended with the filing of charges of illegal paramilitary activity, an episode that is relevant in the present context because it has resulted in serious misinterpretations of the legitimate Swedish resistance organization.

The individual charged was a Swedish national socialist called Otto Hallberg. During the Continuation War in Finland, he had joined the Second Company under Major Malcom Murray and formed the voluntary association Sveaborg, which was named after Sweden's historic coastal fortress near Helsinki. To another former Sveaborg member, who had served in the same company as Hallberg, the association had at first seemed "political only in the sense that it targeted communists" but, with the passage of time, far more "Nazi in its orientation".[30] Sure enough, Sveaborg evolved into a de facto offshoot of Svensk socialistisk samling (SSS), a party led by Swedish Nazi ideologue Sven Olov Lindholm.[31]

However, Hallberg claimed that, since the Prague coup of 1948, his only project had been creating a "community" of citizens who, in the event of a Soviet occupation, would work to evacuate civilians from dangerous areas of Sweden – not "engaging in arms storage or other illegal activities".[32] Citing these claims, Asea director Ragnar Liljeblad argued that Hallberg's organization was more about "evacuation than resistance".[33] Hallberg had contacted him out of the blue with plans for hiding the relatives of Swedish soldiers, primarily women and children, deep in the forest where they could eke out a primitive existence until the country was liberated. Membership in the "community" would only be offered to people who supported Sweden's official policy of neutrality. As the police noted in their report, "Having strong foreign sympathies – of any kind – was regarded as a red flag by those doing the selection of suitable individuals."[34] Hallberg himself was not only anti-communist but deeply anti-American, in line with the resentment felt by many Swedish national socialists at the United States' victorious emergence from the war.[35]

Hallberg's organization, unlike Sveaborg, was otherwise unpolitical. Several soldiers who did not share Hallberg's attitude towards National Socialism had clearly received reassurances about this before they became members.[36] Neither these soldiers nor Liljeblad felt particularly enthusiastic about Hallberg himself. Rather, it was his idea of a rescue organization that they liked – indeed, liked too much to be able to keep it a secret from the Swedish military. When Liljeblad met Chief of the Defence Staff Richard Åkerman at a dinner party, he took the opportunity of mentioning the project and was told to get in touch with a certain "Doctor Palm".[37]

Hallberg himself had opposed contact with official agencies because he feared that if irrelevant bureaucrats, as he regarded them, were given access to the plans for a rescue organization, it would be destroyed by Russian spies "before it ever got off the ground".[38] Hallberg's involvement with Sveaborg had already shown that he enjoyed creating a mystique around his own person and his activities, but he was not wrong about the dangers of being open about the new organization. On 16 May 1952, he was arrested and put in custody.[39]

The police had been tipped off by the civilian security service, which in turn had received a warning from the domestic affairs department of the Defence Staff (where B Bureau would later be established with Birger Elmér as its head). The military's security intelligence service had recruited an informer from among Hallberg's would-be recruits, whose information formed the basis for a classified memo titled "Regarding the preparation of a resistance organization in Sweden".[40] Liljeblad's advances to Richard Åkerman and, subsequently, Thede Palm were thus not the only reason for his arrest. However, that the military's memo reached the security service on 13 May is suggestive and probably not coincidental. The previous day was the first opportunity that Anders Grafström had had to meet Liljeblad and form his own opinion about the suitability of a collaboration, something "he subsequently relayed to General Åkerman".[41] Hallberg was nonetheless acquitted in April 1953 because the court was unable to establish that his activities went beyond merely planning an illegal organization.[42]

---

The initiating of criminal proceedings against Otto Hallberg has been incorrectly interpreted by some commentators as proof that the Swedish state wanted to rid itself of a parallel stay-behind network that it had hitherto tolerated or even collaborated with. Thus, for example, journalist Bosse Schön writes: "Although there is considerable evidence that Hallberg's Nazi-tainted organization was encouraged and supported by the CIA, the American embassy, Sweden's Defence Staff, and circles within the government, it was ultimately unsustainable for Sweden to have two resistance organizations."[43] Daniele Ganser and Mats Deland take a similar line when claiming that the roots of "the Swedish *Stay behind* army can be traced back to a group within the Swedish veterans who participated in the attack on the Soviet Union in 1941–1944 [i.e. Sveaborg]", whose "underground continuation" would be folded into the state-level framework for a Swedish resistance organization that was founded by Anders Grafström.[44]

The explanation offered by journalist Gunnar Wall is, if anything, even more conspiratorial – in light of my review of the primary sources in this chapter – in claiming that Grafström after the war became "a kind of liaison officer for Sveaborg, which thereby found a new patron to replace Hitler".[45] As the criminal investigation of Hallberg makes clear, Grafström poured cold water on the private plans for a resistance organization when he met Hallberg's intermediary Ragnar Liljeblad. "I pointed out," stated Grafström during his interrogation by the police in 1952, "that the challenge of continuing to fight in occupied territory is not just about how to move large parts of Sweden's population into the forest, but considerably more complicated". The police report continued:

> [...] In part, it requires the creation of sabotage groups able to diminish the occupier's capacity to exploit our industries, communications, and so forth. It also requires creating groups that will engage in psychological resistance with a view to strengthening our own will to resist and weakening the enemy. It also means immersing oneself in all the minute problems involved in illegal medical support, document forgery etc., and the acquisition of communications equipment, all of which requires contact

> with the authorities. "An undertaking of this kind must have the full backing of the state."[46]

Thede Palm's diary is concrete evidence that he had no knowledge of Hallberg's initiative. When Palm was shown lists with the names that could be linked to the "Hallberg affair", he told the security service that "none of these names is of someone with whom we have any dealings". According to Palm, Georg Thulin, who directed the security service, was "inclined to think that the man who put them together [Hallberg] was a bit peculiar".[47]

The criminal investigation was nonetheless awkward for the resistance organization. As Palm noted:

> Shaggy Man asked me to come over. He had been summoned by the Minister of the Interior, who had shown him the report on the Liljedahl [i.e. Liljeblad] case. AG [Anders Grafström] seems to have said that an organization existed but added "paid for by the Ministry of the Interior using funds not subject to audit". Everyone is furious.[48]

When Palm himself got hold of the police's interrogation of Grafström, he thought it was "complete madness" and he "proposed various redactions".[49] Fortunately, from Palm's perspective, Grafström had not approved or even read the transcript of the interrogation, the content of which was "substantially rewritten" after he had done so.[50]

The Hallberg incident did have one positive outcome, however, in that it led to a discussion of how to tighten up Sweden's resistance organization and improve its official status. The exposure of Hallberg's organization made Palm, Grafström and Bergkvist anxious that, if asked, they would be unable to produce "any kind of formal authorization".[51] Some time later, Palm recorded in his diary, Minister of the Interior Gunnar Hedlund, who had immediate responsibility in the matter, summoned Lindencrona and requested "documentation on what we had actually been up to" because the Prime Minster "was becoming concerned and wanted to move us all under the control of the Defence Staff".[52] The matter would be decided at the very highest level.

## "A MORE SOLID FOOTING"

"You can see here that the King has signed it. That's the signature of Gustav VI Adolf."[53] Björn von Sydow, political scientist and former Speaker of the Swedish Parliament, points at the sheet of paper that I have placed on the table in front of him, a document neither of us thought existed. It is a decision taken by the State Council to legalize the resistance organization and require auditory oversight of the financial assistance given to it.

My suspicions that this sensational document might exist were first aroused by a note in Tage Erlander's diary about a meeting that took place in summer 1954 between Erlander, Lindencrona, and Arne Geijer, the chairman of Metall who was also one of the sextuplets. In the meeting, Erlander voiced his desire that the resistance organization, if it were to continue its work, be placed under military control. The Hallberg affair was a major factor in his thinking.[54] Yet he was met by fierce protests. "I yielded," Erlander wrote, "but we must at the very least have the King's sanction [...]."[55]

My excitement grew when I discovered that Thede Palm acknowledged Erlander's communication in his diary:

> It was decided that the issue [of the resistance organization] would be raised in a secret session of the State Council. *This means that we have been legalized.* Additionally, the party leaders will be briefed tomorrow. The Prime Minister expressed his satisfaction with our efforts.[56]

But did the plan ever come to anything? When I asked Eric Krönmark, formerly the Minister of Defence, he claimed not to be aware of the existence of any state document about the resistance organization, let alone a decision to legalize it: "I take for granted that it never happened, because in that case it [the founding of such a resistance organization] would have been traceable."[57] Indeed, while serving in the centre-right governments of the 1970s, Krönmark seems to have worried that the resistance organization had a very shaky constitutional basis. He told journalist Mikael Holmström that he felt compelled to attend the meetings of its board "because when you have a group like that operating in the grey zone, there needs to be someone present who has political responsibility and oversight".[58]

Archival research provided no answers – at least initially.

---

A needle in a haystack rarely gets much smaller than a government decision taken in State Council that has been filed away in the National Archives. To find it you need to know in advance not only which department was responsible for the decision but also the date on which the matter was brought up in the Council. Diaries and summary lists of items for discussion are of little help. Things therefore looked hopeless when no decision regarding the resistance movement made around the summer of 1954 could be found where it ought to have been – in the Ministry of the Interior's so-called secret archive. Perhaps it had been destroyed, or perhaps it never got beyond a discussion in the prime minister's office.

I finally found it almost by chance. Filed in the same archive, it was dated December 1955 and titled "Regarding authorization of the Minister of the Interior to appoint a committee for the management of certain activities, etc." The government had directed it to be classified as highly secret and not made available for 50 years, until 2005.[59] Like the title, its contents, for obvious reasons, reveal no more than is absolutely necessary:

> His Majesty the King in Council [the government acting in the King's name], having deemed it necessary that the

> activities which have been carried out within the Ministry of the Interior since 1949, aimed at preparing and securing collaboration and coordination between various groups of Swedish citizens so as to strengthen the realm's defensive capacity in the event of its partial or complete occupation and handle related matters, be established on a more solid footing, hereby authorizes the Minister of the Interior to appoint a committee consisting of the Minister and up to eight additional persons to manage such activities.

The decision further decreed that the total cost of the resistance organization, not to exceed 1,000,000 crowns, should be met by the budget item headed "Costs for special police measures for the prevention and detection of espionage". It also approved "the payments made for these purposes with special authorization from the Prime Minister and the Minister of the Interior for the fiscal years 1951/52, 1952/53, and 1953/54".

For the current fiscal year, the secret committee would receive a maximum of 100,000 crowns, more than ten times the annual salary of a full-time industrial worker in 1955.[60] It would have to submit receipts and an account of how the funds had been spent. The funds would also be subject to audit. (According to a later Council of State decision, this audit was conducted by a senior director of the National Labour Market Board; the decision stipulated that the audit documents "should be burned".[61])

For Björn von Sydow, this document – in contrast to Tage Erlander's four handwritten letters authorizing the formation of a resistance organization in 1949 – proves beyond a doubt that the Swedish resistance organization was legal. "This was a retroactive correction, or tidying-up, of what had gone before," he notes, and adds: "A good decision. It was a reasonable position to take after Stalin's death, when there was perhaps no immediate threat but this [issue of a resistance organization] nonetheless needed to be taken seriously, to continue, and to have what we might call a more legal foundation." Nowadays, von

Sydow observes, it is easy to say that the resistance organization should be formally legalized: "But at that time [during the Cold War] secrecy was essential in order to prevent leaks and mislead potential enemies. Our own media-based view of things just doesn't apply."

According to a contemporary memorandum, this need for secrecy meant that the so-called consultation paper – a preparatory document that likely circulated among the relevant departments prior to the 1955 government decision – was deliberately not saved.[62] Björn von Sydow speculates that the consultation paper may have included a description of the resistance organization's origins, a reference to Erlander's four letters, further details of the financing, and the names of individuals who had already been recruited and in some cases subsequently left. "I think it is entirely reasonable that the consultation paper was destroyed," explains von Sydow: "It would have been dangerous to keep it, particularly if the organization was outlined therein. Leaving a trail for an enemy to follow was simply not an option." He adds, however, that he regards the preservation of the decision itself as "honourable": "It is a significant part of our constitution. If we wanted to do something similar today, we could dig up this sheet of paper and show that such a programme has existed in the past."

The question nonetheless remains: why was this vital knowledge not shared between different governments? Why did Eric Krönmark not know, despite serving as Minister of Defence after responsibility for the resistance organization had been transferred in the late 1960s from the Ministry of the Interior to the Ministry of Defence?[63] In his doctoral dissertation *Life-Line Lost*, security policy researcher Robert Dalsjö has argued that the transfer of knowledge about Sweden's secret military collaboration with the Western powers grew steadily worse during these years. "After [Olof] Palme and [Supreme Commander Lennart] Ljung left the scene in 1986," writes Dalsjö, "hardly anyone in the top political or military leadership was any longer aware that a Plan B for Sweden's security policy had existed."[64]

The primary reason was that the growing strictness of Sweden's neutrality policy increased the political costs of an exposure of its covert security plans, all of which exacerbated fears of a leak. Despite efforts to maintain a strict administrative division – Krönmark called it a Chinese wall – between the resistance organization and Sweden's military collaboration with the West, the two activities naturally overlapped. It is therefore easy to imagine few objections being raised as the government's 1955 decision – one of the few concrete proofs of the existence of a resistance organization with informal links to both the British and American intelligence services – disappeared into the archival shadows. It may be that, as Robert Dalsjö claims, the Swedish military's lifeline to the West was allowed to deteriorate during the 1980s, but the task of maintaining Sweden's resistance organization was taken up by a new generation of members.

# 6

# Vertical Contact

## THE LONE WOLF

The sign on the door read "Operations Office". A fake name intended to sound bland and vaguely bureaucratic or, more plausibly, an appropriation of the Operations Office of the Federation of Swedish Farmers – a non-profit auditing firm for Swedish agricultural workers – as a front for other activities? Whatever the case, the door, which led to a fifth-floor apartment in a pleasant 19th-century building at number 17 on Fleminggatan in the capital's Kungsholmen district, was not meant to pique the interest of unauthorized parties. The small group of individuals permitted to cross its threshold included an insurance adjuster named Gösta Persson, resident in Jämtland County. He visited the apartment many times. An invitation to a meeting at the "Operations Office" on 4 November 1986 – which Gösta has saved even though he ought really to have destroyed both this letter and certain other written communications from the late 1980s – reminds him of the necessity of arriving at exactly the time given, namely 0848hrs in the morning.[1]

What took place in the apartment, like many other related incidents in his life, is still a riddle for Gösta when I meet him in autumn 2022. Or more precisely, when I meet "Felix Thorsell", the false identity that Gösta was expected to adopt every time he entered 17 Fleminggatan. "It was an office building with various authorities, such as the Swedish Forest Agency," says Gösta, who retired years ago, in Swedish that is heavily inflected by the local Jämtland dialect. "The idea was that when you turned up, it looked as though you worked for one of those bodies."[2] He continues: "Directly inside the front door of the apartment was a classroom with three walled cubicles. Sitting in them, we couldn't see each other, only straight ahead. Instead, we had to listen attentively to the others' dialects. 'That must be someone from Värmland,' I remember thinking about a person who sat next to me on one occasion."

Sitting in their separate cubicles, Gösta and the other visitors to the apartment listened to lectures on subjects such as how to create a dead drop or played a kind of strategy game involving different regions of Sweden. Sometimes an instructor, the only person in the room visible from inside the cubicles, came forward and explained the task in more detail. In Gösta's case, it was always about imagining how he might carry out subversive operations in Östergötland County after its occupation. "It was a tricky region to have to train on because it is so different from Jämtland," he says. "I've driven all over Östergötland for that very reason. In my imagination I established a headquarters in the Mo Gård school for the deaf outside Doverstorp, a facility that had greenhouses and sleeping quarters."

At regular intervals, before it was time for the "students" to return to one of the guest apartments that had been placed at their disposal, they were given training exercises around town that could take until the early hours to complete. For instance, they might be asked to fetch a written message that had been rolled up like a cigarette and concealed in a slit in the wall of Stockholm's central rail station, a short distance east of the apartment at 17 Fleminggatan. Gösta remembers these exercises particularly well because he felt that he was being continually observed by invisible eyes in the darkness.

---

If Sweden had been occupied by the Soviet Union during the Cold War, Gösta Persson's mission was to carry out precisely this kind of activity for real in an area that covered two of the five counties that make up the northern region of Norrland, namely Jämtland and Västernorrland. "At the start [of the occupation] we were to lie low and wait for a signal or message," explains Gösta, who was likely given his mission in the early 1970s. The offer came from a lieutenant colonel whom Gösta had got to know through shooting competitions. "I agreed out of weakness – and excitement," he says shyly.

But Gösta's contact with the lieutenant colonel on these matters was quickly replaced by another unknown person, namely the instructor from the secret training site at 17 Fleminggatan. Gösta knew him only as "Anders", probably an assumed name. Anders supplied Gösta with a false identity, "Felix", and gave him some good advice to follow in the event of having to conduct operations for real: "'You only have one friend and it's in your top pocket,'" Gösta remembers him saying, "and he was referring to a cyanide pill". Gösta was entrusted with storing cyanide capsules in a bank deposit box along with plastic explosives and blank passports that could be issued in a false name if needed. Gösta had himself received a false passport that gave his date of birth as 1935, which, he noted with surprise and delight, meant that he was now four years younger. "I was an auditor in a bank so no one ever asked why I was renting a safe deposit box there," he explains.

As time passed, Gösta received more requests to conceal materiel. One day he got a phone call from the train station in Östersund to say that a pallet had arrived for him. "There was a tarpaulin over the pallet with 'Gösta' written on it. I had no idea what was inside, but it turned out to be ammunition for a sub-machine-gun." In the event of occupation, the materiel was to be used above all for sabotaging strategically important targets such as road and train communications that could be used by occupying forces. Gösta had himself identified these targets in advance.

On one occasion in the early 1980s, he convinced his employer, a large insurance company in Jämtland, to sponsor the use of a four-seater Cessna light aircraft to survey elk migration routes that posed a hazard to traffic.[3] He took the opportunity to do some sabotage reconnaissance, photographing a radio mast, various tunnels and bridges, and a railway viaduct on the Inlandsbanan rail network, what one of Sweden's largest daily papers once memorably called "our northerly cardiovascular system".[4] Gösta's undercover directives included making suggestions for escape routes for what he could only say were "important people from Stockholm". They would always be going to England, he adds pensively.

Gösta planned one escape route out of Sweden along the old pilgrim road between Sundsvall on the Baltic coast to Trondheim on Norway's Atlantic seaboard, which he called "From coast to coast". He visualized it as a relay system in which trusted individuals living along the route relieved one another in taking care of the refugees. For example, through his regular work as a claims adjuster, Gösta had got to know a diver who lived on the Norwegian side of the border and who might be useful if he ever had to make his way that far west. Should transportation by sea for some reason become impossible, Gösta had also mapped out 40 or so airfields in the region that could be used for extracting highly important individuals from occupied Swedish territory.

The Norwegian diver was not the only person in Gösta's circle of acquaintance whom he identified as a potential collaborator. Gösta claims to have collected, on his own initiative as well as in response to a request by his contact person Anders, the names of around 50 people in various "zones" of Jämtland and Västernorrland who could potentially be recruited in peacetime. "These were not casual acquaintances but people I knew well. They had to be calm and not overly talkative," he explains, adding: "Farmers were especially well suited because they both knew the terrain and could own land along the pilgrim route. There was no point recruiting city folk." Gösta sent the names of potential recruits to Stockholm for processing by others in the organization. "Not even in a war" would he learn which of them had accepted the invitation, or for that matter who else in the region the organization had already recruited. (The exception being an unnamed radio operator who apparently had a radio apparatus buried somewhere on the island of Frösön, where Jämtland's air wing was at that time based.)

Communication within the network was meant to take place not directly – that is, face to face – but through dead drops. Gösta himself made proposals for such dead drops, including at a number of locations around the Lugnvik district of the city of Östersund. Much later, he learned to his amazement from a work colleague's husband that this man's aged mother had been a secret courier during the Cold War and had known about the dead drops in Lugnvik. Gösta's proposals had evidently met with the approval of those in command.

---

Gösta Persson resigned his position in 1991, the same year that he retired. It was a great relief. "Bearing all that responsibility oneself was heavy," he says with visible emotion. "I was a lone wolf and had no one to consult with. The worst part was thinking about what I would have to do in the event of an occupation. I dreaded it because I was unsure as to whether my plan would actually work. I longed for it [the assignment] to end." Gösta kept these feelings of inadequacy and guilt, which sometimes took the form of unsettling nightmares, to himself until the early 2000s, when he decided to tell his family for the first time about his activities during the Cold War. That is, insofar as those experiences could actually be explained. It had, for example, never been made clear to him which organization he was working for. Reimbursements for trips to Stockholm for training and his consequent loss of income – the only payment ever offered – always took the form of brown envelopes of cash.

When Reinhold Geijer revealed his role as regional leader of Alvar Lindencrona's resistance organization in Jämtland, Härjedalen, Västerbotten and Västernorrland, Gösta immediately suspected that the same network had also recruited him. He still refers to the hotelier in Storlien as his "predecessor", which could well fit time-wise: Geijer was active until 1969.[5] Yet Gösta Persson cannot be wholly certain of where he was in the hierarchy of the stay-behind organization because – as far as he is aware – he was not in command of "one single soul". He has sometimes wondered if there was someone above him. "It's a good thing I saved the letters, so that nobody can question that I was actually involved," he concludes.

## "TWO HUNDRED MEN UNDER MY COMMAND"

The Norsholm estate lies between Norrköping and Linköping, more than 700km from Östersund. When I visit in spring 2022, it is still owned by Pehr Löfgreen, a former member of parliament for the Moderate Party who has managed the estate since he came of age in 1955.* "Because my father was ill, I was given a great deal of responsibility for Norsholm from an early age," explains Pehr, adding: "I have been a farmer my entire life and have farmed the largest holdings in all Östergötland."[6] By the end of the 1960s, according to a contemporary newspaper article, he owned and leased more than 600 hectares.[7]

Pehr seems to remember that it was when he took over running the estate that an acquaintance asked if he was interested in becoming involved in a Swedish resistance organization to oppose a Soviet occupation. "I accepted because I had a big head

* Pehr Löfgreen passed away on 6 September 2022.

and I felt honoured," says Pehr in a playful tone that reflects his slightly subversive personality – a personality that accounts for why he was only allowed to represent the Moderate Party in the Swedish parliament for one term of office, between 1991 and 1994. He continues in a more serious voice:

> I felt that a resistance organization was necessary for the future, and I was informed that I was deemed suitable because I had a large network of contacts and a background in the military. Father [Captain Helmer Löfgreen] was a career officer in the infantry in Linköping and I did my military service in the cavalry in Skövde and Umeå.

Pehr says that he was appointed regional commander of the "eastern region" with the inconspicuous codename "Lars Nilsson". He was relieved of this command at the end of the Cold War and received as a gesture of thanks some 18th-century glasses from the Reijmyre glassworks in Östergötland bearing the monogram of King Gustav III. "Our mission was to work within this region for the liberation of Sweden," he explains: "It involved partisan warfare and the evacuation of key individuals in the region, possibly to an overseas destination." As regional commander he was required to establish a headquarters in Östergötland; Norsholm, with its large holdings, was the natural choice. He stored pistols and sub-machine-guns there. "I still have a weapon in the attic," says Pehr. He was also expected to maintain communications with other resistance men in the region. "At one point I had two hundred men under my command. Many of them, those whom I knew to be stable individuals, were recruited by me personally," he relates. "These were ordinary people, neither communists nor Nazis, who had bona fide reasons for moving about. Travelling salesmen were ideal."

According to Pehr, these individuals were divided into what he estimates at around 40 smaller groups or cells, none of whom were supposed to know about the others' existence. "Orders came from above, from the central level, about how the cells should be organized, and they were of different sizes," he says. "The smaller the cell, the better." But not all recruits were told that they had been selected for a resistance organization intended to mobilize in the event of an occupation. "It varied from case to case," says Pehr, who only informed those whom he could fully trust. In peacetime his primary means of communication with the cells was by dead drops. Pehr relates that there was a concealed dead drop on the bridge over the Motala River where messages were regularly deposited and collected: "Many of the letters were very strange."

---

Few people knew about Pehr's mission – not even his friend in the Moderate Party, Eric Krönmark, although the latter was unsurprised when he did finally learn about it. Krönmark accounts for his lack of surprise by the fact that his party comrade held a "leading position in Östergötland".[8] Pehr himself is certain that he was working for the Swedish stay-behind organization. He describes how he once met Alvar Lindencrona, albeit with only a "vague notion" of the other's role in the resistance organization. "It was just general talk. He [Lindencrona] was very sociable," Pehr recalls of the meeting.

Later, Pehr came into contact with Curt-Steffan Giesecke. Pehr claims that because Giesecke knew that Pehr and his wife owned an apartment in Spain, he asked Pehr to verify a report that Russian spy Stig Bergling had been seen in an officers' club in the Canary Islands after his highly publicized escape from Sweden in 1987. Bergling, who had worked on registering secret documents for the security service and had been previously employed at the Defence Staff's security division, was regarded as a severe threat to Swedish defence interests – including the resistance organization. "Bergling was assumed to have insider knowledge of our activity, so we had to reorganize it," Giesecke told journalist Mikael Holmström.[9] A third person whom Pehr Löfgreen claims to have met during his time in the resistance organization was Anders Grafström, the "top dog" on the organization's operative side.

Among his other duties Grafström gave talks about "threat scenarios and possible outcomes" on the courses in Stockholm that Pehr periodically received an honorarium and travel expenses to attend. He faintly remembers that these were associated with an address on Bergsgatan, a street in the central district of Kungsholmen, but is careful to point out that the resistance organization often changed premises. It was here Pehr believes that he met other regional heads. "But we sat behind curtains and could not see each other. This practice went on for a very long time." On these training courses Pehr had the "honour" of spending the night in other apartments at the disposal of the resistance organization, including one on Sturegatan, an upscale address in the central district of Östermalm. On occasion he was accompanied by his wife Helen, who quickly chimes in: "He knew that I could keep quiet." When I tell the couple that in spring 2022 I was myself living on Fleminggatan, in the Kungsholmen district, Pehr remarks unprompted: "The organization had an apartment there, too."

## THE VEIL IS TORN

It is not uncommon for covert operations to use safe houses. The intelligence service T Bureau, for example, initially had at its disposal apartments under the names of "G. Berggren" and "Technical Analysis", and in mid-1948 "moved to an apartment at 58B Sturegatan (first floor), whose previous tenant [...] had gone by the thoroughly creditable name 'The 1948 Registration Form Committee'".[10] Jan Leijonhielm, who worked at IB, the successor to T Bureau, explains how such arrangements often worked: "Basically, the official owner is not the state or an intelligence service but a front of some kind."[11]

Leijonhielm's own workplace, the foreign section of IB, was housed in a front-owned apartment at 24 Grevgatan in the

Östermalm district. "In that instance the house was owned by an acquaintance of [Birger] Elmér, but the brothers [Jonas and Robert] af Jochnick and their cosmetics company Oriflame contributed the signage," he explains. Similarly, the door to the IB headquarters, which lay nearby at 56 Valhallavägen and were known internally as Central, bore a name plate that read "FortF" – short for Fortifikationsförvaltningen, the army's Fortification Administration.[12] In 1968, author and slavicist Bengt Jangfeldt did his military service at the Defence Staff in what was later revealed to be another of IB's safe houses, also located on Östermalmsgatan and with a typical Swedish name on the door.[13]

In the case of the resistance organization, the central office seems at first to have been located in an apartment at 16 Bergsgatan in the capital's Kungsholmen district.[14] According to Reinhold Geijer, who paid several visits to the head office, it contained four radio operators, who took turns to maintain radio readiness. "They were always there whenever you entered the premises on Bergsgatan and still there whenever you left," explains Geijer in interview notes preserved in the archive of journalist Thomas Kanger.[15] The office also had a "materiel administrator" and "a few civilians with cover names" whom Geijer "greeted discreetly". In autumn 2024, when I visited what seems likely to have been the apartment in question, it is clear that it could well have been used by the resistance organization.[16] Comprising six large rooms on the building's fourth floor, the apartment has a rambling layout with many corridors and doors that could easily be partitioned into discreet sections without it being obvious to a visitor.

At some point – it is unclear when exactly – the office moved from Bergsgatan. Curt-Steffan Giesecke told journalist Mikael Holmström that during his time as its commander, the resistance organization offered "advanced training at its premises on Fleminggatan, close to [insurance company] Trygg-Hansa" where Giesecke was managing director between 1978 and 1986.[17]

When Giesecke expanded on these memories, he explained that the resistance organization's office was "at [the intersection between Fleminggatan and] Scheelegatan, on the opposite corner from Trygg-Hansa".[18] If correct, it can refer to only one address: 17 Fleminggatan. If you stand against its front door you have an unimpeded view of Trygg-Hansa's brutalist glass-and-brick headquarters at 18–20 Fleminggatan across the street.[19]

Today, as it has for some time, 17 Fleminggatan comprises both residential apartments and offices. In the late 1970s and early 1980s, it was home to the Swedish Fire Association's Electrical Committee and the Swedish Association for Health and Exercise.[20] While both were legitimate organizations, their names could also have served as covers for a secret resistance organization in the same vein as "Operations Office". Admittedly, Giesecke faintly remembers the office at Fleminggatan having had a "common surname" on its front door.[21] But this does not necessarily mean that the resistance organization's head office was located elsewhere. On the contrary, the combination of Giesecke's topographical description and Gösta Persson's written invitation requires us to exclude that possibility.

"Operations Office" may have been a designation that was only used occasionally, such as on training days, so that participants, should they ever return on their own initiative, would be uncertain which apartment they had entered. (Moreover, by putting up a temporary sign moments before a specified arrival time and then removing it as soon as participants had arrived, there would be no danger of arousing the postal worker's curiosity.) Such speculation finds support in the fact that IB chief Birger Elmér in 1973 established an office under the name "CGB Company" at 5 Rindögatan in the Gärdet district of Stockholm, but the name on its front door was simply "Friberg" – the surname of Elmér's secretary.[22] Other explanations are also possible, such as that Giesecke simply misremembered, or that the resistance organization had several apartments in the same building.

Whatever the case, Gösta Persson's claim to have been recruited by Sweden's stay-behind organization can be considered as verified. Further support comes from the fact that courses similar to those described by Gösta were arranged by Norway's equivalent organization, which used "ex-Linge [unit] people" as instructors.[23] The similarities between Gösta's testimony and Pehr Löfgreen's – above all, the curious and important detail that participants in resistance organization courses were physically separated and prevented from seeing each other – likewise support the latter's account.

---

We find additional confirmation that both men were part of the resistance organization in documents, now also preserved in journalist Thomas Kanger's archive, that came to light following the death of a confirmed regional commander. The person in question was a company commander and businessman from the Småland region of Sweden whose daughters did not want either his or their own names to be published when the newspaper *Dagens Nyheter* first revealed the story in 1998. Out of respect for their wishes, I will refer to this director, whom I have identified, as "A. J."

According to A. J.'s handwritten notes about his life, after the end of the war in 1945 he began to be troubled by the idea of a Soviet occupation of Sweden and the threat of his country sharing the fate of states in Central and Eastern Europe, "crippled and terrorized by communist quislings entirely dependent on the interests of their Soviet leaders".[24] A. J. "brooded incessantly" about how he personally would – and should – respond in such a situation. In his imagination he planned "a tiny organization entirely under the control of the government in exile" that could offer resistance to the occupying forces. He sought out potential collaborators "mostly from among commercial travellers, their assistants, forestry workers, and rangers and the like, all of the old school".

One day in 1951, his daydreams suddenly became a reality. A. J. received a startling letter from a Major Anders Grafström, adjutant to the Chief of the Army at the Defence Staff in Stockholm:

> Through one of my fellow officers I have heard of your interest in Sweden's defence problems – and not merely those of the present moment. I would value very highly an opportunity to discuss with you certain circumstances that may prove decisive in the future.[25]

The upshot of the meeting with Grafström was that A. J., who by his own admission had hitherto only "'toyed' with the idea of an area with a radius of 70 kilometres", was given formal responsibility for preparing civilian resistance in a region that included "Småland, Östergötland, and a little more besides".[26]

A. J. was expected to reconnoitre the entire area himself, which he managed to the best of his ability under the cover of his well-known interests in car and orienteering races and local history. He correctly guessed that his wife, who had only minimal knowledge of his activities, would not be puzzled by his growing interest in "churches, local history sites and museums, and beauty spots when we went for Sunday drives – drives that grew progressively longer". According to *Dagens Nyheter*, A. J.'s children suspected absolutely nothing. "All those Sunday excursions – I thought they were for our sake," explained one of his daughters, who admitted that she had mixed feelings about her father's secret assignment.[27]

In a letter to an unknown correspondent from 1953, A. J. describes the fruits of these covert reconnaissance activities:

> For the past few months I have been using my little leisure time to familiarize myself generally with the *competition*

> *area*. I have yet to cover the area around Kalmar and e[ast] of Norrköping. My guess is that there is no more suitable area south of the Dal River than that of Södra Östergötland, Jönköping, and Kalmar counties. From Lake Vättern to the Baltic Sea there is a single area in which thousands of partisans and others could operate while remaining concealed with the help of loyal civilians, such that no power on earth could destroy or disable them.[28]

Other letters also indicate that A. J., during the period of his active involvement, which extended at least into the 1960s, made relatively comprehensive preparations in his region; Reinhold Geijer would later claim that they exceeded his own.[29] Among other things, A. J. designated preliminary storage depots and drop zones where Allied aircraft could deliver materiel to the resistance organization. He even drew up long lists with the names of individuals whose potential suitability for carrying out tasks for the resistance organization "should be investigated", complete with descriptions of their relevant personality traits. For example, A. J. described a colleague at his own company as "energetic, intelligent, cool-headed, and calculating". Another person, an engineer with a prosthetic hand who worked in manufacturing, was set down as "a man to rely on".[30]

From an archival sources perspective, however, the most important of the documents preserved by A. J. is one codenamed "Plan Maize", which apparently outlines the structure of the entire regional resistance organization.[31] The plan, which does not identify its author, seems to have been partly inspired by the contemporary military-territorial division of Sweden into decentralized "mil-divs" or military divisions, which in the event of war would be able to fight independently of the Defence Staff leadership in Stockholm. At the top of the organization chart is a function referred to simply as "mil-div head", which should of course be understood as the standard designation in the resistance organization of "regional commander" or "RC".[32]

Next in the regional chain of command are a number of "rye districts", which the document indicates correspond to home guard circuits. As with the home guard, these are under the command of a district commander, whose duties include the storage of various kinds of materiel: chemicals, tinned food, weapons, etc. The district is in turn in charge of a number of smaller groups, each comprising around five men, including a leader. These so-called "potato groups" are equipped with plastic explosives, primer cartridges and fuses. The plan stipulates that "District R" and "P Groups" are to "work in ignorance of each other". "P staff" – that is, the members of the individual cell – are expected to "work for the most part without knowledge of each other".

This way of organizing covert activities, Thede Palm explains in his book on the subject, is called a "vertical" arrangement of contacts.[33] In order to minimize the risk of betrayal and discovery, members communicate for the most part upwards or downwards in the organization, not "horizontally" on the same level. In this choice of organizational form, the Swedish resistance organization resembles the "group organizations" of C Bureau, as here described by Gellert Hardi-Kovacs:

> Each group organization was to be directed by a group leader. Under him there would be a deputy leader and various district leaders, each of which managed a smaller and restricted part of the group organization's area of responsibility. In turn, the group organization had a coordinator at C Bureau's head office, known as the head of section. The head of section was to be in continual contact with the group leader out in the field, analyse and process their information and communicate to them the bureau leadership's directives.[34]

Further parallels emerge between the Cold War resistance organization and World War II-era group organizations, of which the "homeland stewards" formed a part, when Hardi-Kovacs explains that the head of section was also responsible for providing training to selected personnel:

> These training courses were arranged in Stockholm as well as in the [personnel's own] operating area. They took place at regular intervals and helped personnel to feel that they were part of a dynamic organization that was continually developing.[35]

The principle of vertical contact shared by C Bureau and "Plan Maize" runs throughout Gösta Persson's and Pehr Löfgreen's inside accounts of the Swedish resistance organization. This makes it easier to formulate a plausible description of their respective functions.

Pehr Löfgreen was indeed most likely a regional commander. Like the businessman A. J., he was in direct contact with, and can identify by name, individuals in the resistance organization's national leadership. He also definitely knows that he was responsible for a sprawling network of cells. However, given that A. J. was clearly put in charge of a region that included Östergötland, it is possible that Löfgreen (who was 88 years old when I interviewed him) made a mistake about when exactly he became regional commander. It was perhaps not when he turned 21 – the age of majority in Sweden in 1955 – and took over the running of Norsholm, but rather some time after his father's death in 1967, by which time Löfgreen was well established in the local area and had built a larger network of contacts.[36] Another possibility is that A. J., feeling overwhelmed by the task of drawing up detailed plans for the huge area for which he was responsible, concentrated all his efforts on his home county of Småland.[37] Theoretically, A. J. and Pehr Löfgreen could also have worked in parallel for a while, so that the latter could have a probationary period as regional commander.

Gösta Persson's place in the organization is harder to determine. His own best guess is that he replaced Reinhold Geijer, and the experiences that he describes certainly bear a strong resemblance to the regional commander's duties and communication channels within the organization. But there are also significant differences – and, not least, his description of himself as a "lone wolf" – which make me think that Persson was lower down in the hierarchy than regional commander. Geijer, it is true, also felt alone in Storlien in the Jämtland mountains and Thomas Kanger's interview notes record that he said it was "not at all like it was for A. J." in the south.[38] (He was also a doubter, someone who questioned his psychological preparedness to lead his resistance groups while "surrounded by Russians".) Yet Geijer, like A. J., was not a solitary figure isolated in the resistance organization. He knew full well what kind of organization he was working for and was even personally acquainted with several of his superiors.

Significantly, when Geijer turned 50 in March 1967, he was given a full-blown "birthday parade" outside his apartment in Stockholm, as a contemporary newspaper reported:

> Among those carrying Swedish flags in the procession could be seen Lieutenant General Gustaf Dyrssen, Major General Malcolm Murray, Colonel Anders Grafström, royal caterer Tore Wretman, Volvo director Hans Blenner, and many others of the honoree's closest friends. [...] Earlier in the day, director Geijer had received gifts including an exquisite silver cigarette case from Crown Prince Carl Gustaf and his four sisters.[39]

Gösta Persson may instead have been at either the "rye" level of district head or the "potato" level of cell leader, in which case the man he knew as Anders would have been a handler, akin to the trained instructors who were parachuted into resistance cells during World War II.[40] When I put "Plan Maize" on the table in front of Gösta, he notes with surprise that the phrase "potato group" sounds familiar: "It's almost as though I'm going back in time... It feels like I thought it was an odd phrase."

# 7

# *Vivat Carolus Rex Sueciæ*

## BORN ON THE FIRST OF MAY

No one in Sweden before or since has ever had the first name Curt-Steffan. Not surprisingly, Curt-Steffan Giesecke was always known as "Curre". "I once asked my grandmother where she had got the name from, but she couldn't remember," relates Curt-Steffan's son Johan, once a national epidemiologist but now retired from medicine, as we look at the family's paintings in his country house, where the celebrated Swedish children's author Elsa Beskow once spent her summers.[1]

The unusual name did not prove to be a handicap to Curt-Steffan Giesecke. At the age of 26, he was recruited by the Swedish Employers' Confederation (SAF); at 32, he became its deputy director and, at 45, its managing director. As Johan explains, this made his father one of a handful of men "who set the salaries for all Swedes": "In the negotiating model that governed the Swedish labour market, three people from SAF and three from the Trade Union Confederation (LO) agreed on the salaries of industrial workers, which shaped in turn the salaries of everyone else in work." Working for SAF was Curt-Steffan Giesecke's main mission in life, one that he regarded as benefitting the entire country.

As Giesecke's son explains, this patriotic sense of duty was a more important driving force than personal prestige or economic gain: "He was the ideal Swedish official: impeccably honest, impartial, discreet, and reliable." It is easy to see how these qualities would have been invaluable resources for the delicate mission that Giesecke was tasked with while serving as an infantryman during World War II, namely to ensure that German soldiers did not cross the national border painted on the floor of the train carriages of injured German soldiers as they transited on Swedish railways.[2]

They may also have been invaluable for writing satirical and political detective novels under a pseudonym. For it has been speculated that Curt-Steffan Giesecke was the real person behind the nom de plume Bo Balderson, whose identity continues to baffle Swedish cultural commentators today. By coincidence, Balderson's novels were published by Åke Runnquist at Albert Bonniers förlag, who had been a close friend of Giesecke's since their schooldays. While on foreign holidays, both men, to the frustration of their wives, used to spend considerable time writing limericks to each other about the places they were visiting. They even published a collection of limericks under the pseudonyms Ture Seck and Rune Åqvist. Did their collaboration extend to writing detective novels together?[3]

If so, it would have allowed Giesecke to avoid lying when, with a mixture of amusement and playfulness, he denied being Bo Balderson in a radio interview in 2009. On the same occasion he also answered the question of whether it was difficult for Balderson to be alone with his secret: "I can think of weighty matters that would be difficult to carry around on one's own, but the authorship of a few books is surely something that one could manage."[4] Giesecke did not specify what "weighty matters" he had in mind, but his own involvement in the Swedish resistance organization is an obvious candidate. As his son Johan explains, he never shared his secret with his family during all the time he was active.

One of the few times that Johan heard his father refer to resistance work was when Reinhold Geijer made his public appearance. "He talks too much," remarked Giesecke tersely.

---

In a coincidence that seems almost too good to be true, Giesecke was born on 1 May, the workers' day, and spent his first year living in the building that is now the Stockholm headquarters of Sweden's LO. During all his years as director of SAF, he enjoyed good personal relationships with his counterparts in the labour movement: Arne Geijer and his successor as LO chairman, Gunnar Nilsson. Geijer even visited Giesecke at the family's summer house on the island of Sydkoster on Sweden's west coast. The labour movement's travel agency, Reso, owned a guest house on the neighbouring island of Nordkoster. "In those days they were real pals," says Johan Giesecke gently.[5]

Curt-Steffan Giesecke's relationship with Gunnar Nilsson was less friendly, but when asked by an interviewer from the trade union confederation magazine in 1993 how he would have handled Sweden's unemployment crisis if he had still been SAF's managing director, he replied in terms that illustrate the ease with which the two men had cooperated: "I would have given Gunnar a call and said, 'Let's sit down and talk through these problems without any prior conditions and see what we can do.'" "And I would have said yes," added Nilsson with a laugh.[6] Indeed, there were those on the employers' side who felt that Giesecke's relationship with the labour movement was too friendly, something that ultimately led to controversy over his position at SAF. "Large portions of Swedish industry saw Father as too soft on LO," says Johan. "Above all, the big players in manufacturing, Asea and Volvo, were unhappy about 'paying too much attention to the socialists.' This led to them lobbying for [Asea managing director] Curt Nicolin to become chair of SAF's board, and then eventually pushing Father out entirely."[7] After

Giesecke's departure, SAF adopted a more confrontational and neoliberal attitude, which resulted in the Moderate Party and other centre-right parties close to SAF reinventing themselves in the same style.

Can this development, which would have profound consequences for Swedish politics, be separated from Giesecke's involvement in the resistance organization? No one else in the SAF leadership knew about Giesecke's secret collaboration for Sweden's national interest with Arne Geijer and Gunnar Nilsson, who also succeeded Geijer on the board of the resistance organization.[8] As a result, the diplomacy and mutual understanding that characterized the collaboration, which doubtless left its mark on their negotiations about the labour market, could be regarded by critics as weakness, if not outright submissiveness. After Giesecke was edged out as director in 1978, taking with him his knowledge of the real reasons, his critics in industry felt at liberty to abandon the corporatist state. Of course, it could be countered that SAF's new militancy in the 1970s was merely the symptom of a larger systemic shift, ushered in by social democracy's politicization of the labour market earlier in the decade.[9] But the loss of the Swedish resistance organization's influence as a unifying force on capital and organized labour may well have been a contributing factor.

This proposition finds support in the fact that a similar development seems to have taken place within LO with the replacement of Gunnar Nilsson in the early 1980s by Stig Malm, who, unlike his predecessor as chairman, was not initiated into the resistance organization.[10] "During Stig's time, the prevailing mood was anything but one of friendly agreement," recalls Göran Tunhammar, who himself knew nothing of the resistance organization when he took over as SAF managing director in 1990. "He could kick over chairs, rush out of the room and slam the door. Things were lousy but the relationship with LO improved again during Bertil's time."[11] Bertil Jonsson, as noted earlier, had been informed of the resistance organization's existence while he was still Malm's deputy chairman. As a result, the second-generation resistance organization, which was led by Giesecke after his tenure at SAF, operated outside the formal structures of the labour market to a far greater degree than the first generation had done. Some time around 1995 or later, a third generation of resistance organization operatives – now even more distant from its corporatist roots – began under the leadership of former Chief of the Home Guard Robert Lugn, father of the prominent playwright and poet Kristina Lugn.[12] By this point, Giesecke had resigned his position.

Giesecke has himself stated that he was personally thanked by Minister of Defence Thage G. Peterson and was presented with "a pair of cufflinks with the emblem of the armed forces".[13] But he also received another retirement present, quite unexpected from a Social Democratic government, if it was indeed the giver. Johan Giesecke and his wife Kajsa show me three small handmade glasses that appeared at the family's summer house on Koster island at around this time in the mid-1990s and that his father Curt-Steffan claimed to have received as a thank you for his contributions to the resistance organization. Each of the glasses, which come from Reijmyre glassworks in Östergötland, is engraved with the words *Vivat Carolus Rex Suecia*: Long Live King Carl of Sweden.

## RESISTANCE AFTER THE WALL

Several other sources indicate that by 1995 Curt-Steffan Giesecke had been replaced as head of the Swedish resistance organization. "It didn't happen during the [Carl] Bildt government [of 1991–94]," claims Ingemar Engman, who for many years served as a key intermediary between the Social Democrats, the intelligence service, and the Ministry of Defence.[14] Giesecke himself also stated that he never had any contact with the centre-right government's Minister of Defence Anders Björck; by contrast, he often met with Björck's predecessor, the Social Democrat Roine Carlsson, "in a special room at the top of the ministry building".[15]

The change of leadership in the resistance organization must therefore have taken place after the transition from the centre-right government in October 1994. Thage G. Peterson, who took over as Minister of Defence in the incoming Social Democratic government, thinks this likely:

> I knew [Curt-Steffan] Giesecke well, of course, and so can't exclude – it's even quite plausible – that I knew he was going to resign [as head of the resistance organization]. I made a point of knowing about what fell under my area of responsibility. But I can't confidently say more than that, given that I'm now over ninety.[16]

An additional source confirms the latest date for Giesecke's tenure as head of the organization. When former National Police Commissioner Björn Eriksson left the board of the resistance organization in 1996, following his appointment as Governor of Östergötland County, Giesecke had already left. Eriksson confirmed as much himself when he gave me what was his first interview about working for the resistance organization.

---

At our meeting in autumn 2022, Björn Eriksson felt less constrained by the informal promises he had once given never to speak about the resistance organization: "The passage of time tends to remove the need for secrecy and in its technical aspects the subject has ceased to be of immediate relevance."[17] He also believes that Sweden's current decision-makers can learn from how he and others in the resistance organization reasoned, more than three decades ago: "The person who contemplates the unthinkable right from the start always has a certain advantage," remarks Eriksson, who became involved in the resistance organization sometime around 1989–90. "That's how I remember it. I was appointed National Police

Commissioner in 1988 and clearly people watched me for a while and concluded that someone like Eriksson would fit in. In those days, the National Police Commissioner was also head of the security service."

However, according to Eriksson, other factors were involved in his selection:

> Presumably I had also gained a certain amount of respect for playing it close to the chest. It was very obvious that certain individuals who would have been eligible on the basis of their position in society were not let in because of concerns about their lack of discretion. You can be on the right team but still be the wrong person if you can't hold your tongue.

Eriksson was recruited not to a board but to what he describes as a "discussion group" comprising around ten people. As he explains:

> Some of them I knew, others were complete strangers. We had conversations along the lines of: "What would be the smart thing to do [during an occupation], what pitfalls should we avoid, and what resources do we have?" It felt right, it felt patriotic. [...] But we weren't a bunch of old men sitting around planning operations or running about leaving messages in dead drops. Not at my level, at least. I've never taken part in any practical exercises.

The only activities of this kind that Eriksson can remember were discussions about how the resistance organization could practice, in a discreet and appropriate fashion, using its communications equipment. "One problem was that open agencies [i.e. police] were often nearby, such as at Arlanda airport [in Stockholm], and we were anxious to avoid causing any kind of collision. A resistance organization has nothing to gain by becoming known to large numbers of people, because the risk of infiltration increases."

For Eriksson, training to be able to communicate with surviving Western democracies following a Russian invasion was in fact the core of the resistance organization's activities. "I never felt that it was about fighting," he explains, but adds as a qualifier that he was never familiar with the organization as a whole. "The whole idea was that even those at the top would never be able to see everything. I only knew about my little corner. *Need to know* is one of the soundest principles there is, and it is the cornerstone of all intelligence work." He goes on: "The political leadership didn't need to know everything, either. In the first place, they wouldn't have survived in the most probable scenario, and in the second, the organization never engaged in activity that was illegal in any sense of the word."

According to his own estimate, Eriksson's main task in the resistance organization was to be ready to exploit his contact network, which at that time reached far into the various structures of law enforcement in the West. As he explains:

> Had there been an occupation, I knew 200–300 key individuals in the worlds of open and covert policing; I was even president of Interpol. This could have been useful if I had been fortunate enough to escape being picked off at a very early stage of an occupation. [...] Those of us who remained would have represented the last avenue for communicating with the outside world and relaying what was happening in Sweden.

This line of reasoning recalls an old statement by Minister of Defence Sven Andersson about how important it is that prominent Swedes cultivate their overseas relationships against the possibility of an emergency situation: "Having good personal contacts is key, because if Sweden goes under, it's the only thing that will help."[18]

If the recruiting of Björn Eriksson was, to use his own words, above all "an investment in a contact network", he believes that the other members of the resistance network filled slightly different functions. As he explains:

> It was a marker of the good intentions [of the organization] that the whole business was managed by representatives of the unions and the employers, who worked a bit like marriage makers or high priests. It would have seemed more suspicious if people in floppy hats and trench coats with a cigarette dangling from the corner of their mouths had come up and said, "Let's all join forces against the dreaded enemy."

When asked whether it made sense for the Swedish resistance movement to remain active in the mid-1990s – years after the fall of the Berlin Wall and the collapse of the USSR – Eriksson replies: "The Cold War had been going on since the 1940s, so just because a wall came down didn't mean that everything changed overnight." He adds: "We had no way of knowing the future, and when you are the chief of police your starting point always has to be that there is some new devilry waiting round the corner." Others, however, would have more optimistic expectations.

## "ROMANTICIZING RESISTANCE"

"I had never heard of the stay-behind programme before a colonel told us in the Defence Commission about it in 1991, but then it was more about tidying away old stuff."[19] The speaker is Michael Sahlin, who as State Secretary to the Minister of Defence headed the Defence Commission tasked with preparing the groundwork for the 1992 government decision on defence spending. According to a contemporary news article, the decision was intended to "set out Sweden's long-term security policy and defence alignments up until the year 2002".[20] It was within the context of this work that Sahlin learned for the first time that "there was a function, a bag of money, and a plan" for dealing with an occupation of Sweden. But no sooner had the Defence Commission been made aware of these facts than its members decided that the resistance movement was "obsolete".

Sahlin remembers clearly how the matter was discussed by the Defence Commission:

> A Social Democratic politician talked scornfully about "romanticizing resistance". But, as chairperson, I also felt that we did not need to sit around making contingency plans for an occupation now that the Cold War had ended. What exactly had gone on [in the resistance movement] was never properly established: it was seen as a relic of the past.

Unsurprisingly, the 1992 government decision on defence spending included the cancellation of Sahlin's "bag of money" to the resistance organization. "Speculating about and preparing for the worst case scenario – occupation – felt contrived and out of place," he adds. "The Minister of Defence [Anders Björck] and the Prime Minister [Carl Bildt] took the same view."

The Government Offices of the Moderate Party-led coalition henceforth made no effort towards wartime contingency planning, recalls Peter Egardt, who served as State Secretary to the Prime Minister during the entire period of centre-right government from 1991 to 1994, and was also the highest ranking official with responsibility for security matters.[21] For example, Egardt explains, there was no plan for establishing a Swedish government in exile in the event of an attack on the country. Instead, Sweden's senior cabinet ministers sat in a bunker and practised *receiving* Baltic governments in exile and refugees, on the assumption that Russia would launch a revanchist coup attempt against one of Sweden's eastern neighbours. Of one thing everyone was now certain: war could never again come to Sweden.

# Epilogue

## THE RESISTANCE ORGANIZATION – THE EMPIRICAL EVIDENCE

Any investigation into a phenomenon that a country's political and military leadership have cloaked in secrecy will necessarily be somewhat motley and fragmentary. For this reason it may be worth reviewing preceding chapters' key findings with regard to Sweden's resistance organization and its preparations for a potential Soviet occupation during the Cold War.

In the broadest terms, we can say that this was not a matter of some loosely affiliated network operating without an institutional footing. On the contrary, the resistance organization, which was established in 1949 at the behest of Prime Minister Tage Erlander and led by representatives of the Swedish trade union movement, agricultural organizations and private employers, should be understood as the exact counterpart of the corporately organized bodies in the fields of labour and social policy, such as the National Labour Market Board (AMS), which was established in 1947. The purpose of giving board seats to representatives from the labour movement and the Employers' Confederation was to establish a broad base of legitimacy for activities that would affect the lives of all citizens. That these parties would have played similar roles in the event of an occupation by providing a popular base for the

Swedish resistance movement is confirmed by several people in this book, including Göran Tunhammar, former managing director of the Swedish Employers' Confederation, and former National Police Commissioner Björn Eriksson.

The resistance organization thus confirms historian Niklas Stenlås's acute observation that Sweden's corporative welfare state and its similarly expansive national defence counterpart – its Cold War-era state of readiness, so to speak – reflected and, in some measure, shaped each other.[1] Yet the resistance organization was not a public body in the narrow sense of the word. Rather, the fact that it relied on a nationwide structure of cells, whose largely volunteer membership comprised low-ranking officials, farmers and small entrepreneurs, means that it genuinely warrants the designation of a *movement*.

However, there is no firm data on how many people were involved in this movement. In December 1950, Thede Palm learned from Norway's intelligence director Vilhelm Evang that around 1,000 individuals had been "approached" about joining the corresponding organization in Norway. "Evang estimated," wrote Palm in his diary, "that establishing something equivalent for us [in Sweden] would mean approaching about 2,500 people."[2] Yet it is unlikely that Palm and the other men in the operative leadership of the Swedish resistance organization really contemplated recruiting so many people: maintaining secrecy would have been wholly unfeasible. It is quite conceivable, however, that Evang's estimate of the numbers needed in Sweden corresponds roughly to what the resistance organization expected to be able to mobilize in the event of an occupation, given that it had already recruited key individuals with extensive networks in the Swedish countryside, who in turn were on the lookout for suitable recruits if the situation became critical. Having a larger cadre of wartime personnel would have all but guaranteed infiltration by the enemy.

The chameleon-like character of the resistance organization – half state-run and half civilian – eventually gained a legal foundation thanks to a hitherto unknown government decision, taken in 1955 in accordance with the constitution and in the presence of King Gustaf VI Adolf. The decision, which described an entity that was already in existence, approved the resistance organization *ex post facto*, thereby resolving an awkward state of affairs in which the organization's only official sanction had been a few letters of authorization signed by the Prime Minister.

In Norway, there was no equivalent "*stay-behind* law" that "gave *direct* and *unquestioning* support for the establishment of a secret, preparatory defence organization as part of national contingency planning".[3] During the Cold War, individual members of the Norwegian resistance organization would have been liable to criminal penalties if they had been exposed in peacetime and arrested for planning paramilitary activities. Not so in Sweden, where the resistance organization, as we now know, was also a legally defined and thus formally legitimate *organization*.

The purpose of this organization was to prepare and manage what we might call, borrowing a phrase from peace and conflict researcher Wilhelm Agrell, "well-organized defeat".[4] Were Sweden to be occupied, strategic hubs for civil resistance in the form of local headquarters, radio transmission sites and dead drops would already have been set up or decided upon, along with escape routes, hiding places for key decision-makers, and suitable arrangements for free Swedish media. If the worst were to happen, preparations would also have been made for partisan warfare and the sabotage of vital parts of the country's infrastructure. It would been unreasonable to expect the resistance organization to handle all these tasks simultaneously and under all circumstances; in an acute situation, it would doubtless have had to adapt and make priorities. Nonetheless, the plan was that the resistance organization should have a wide range of capabilities.

As we now know, the resistance organization was entirely Swedish and not, as has often been claimed, a creation of NATO. In addition to the fact that in its composition the organization owed far more to Sweden's AMS entity than to the Western military alliance NATO, it was always under Swedish command. An early attempt by the British and the Americans to take control of the resistance organization was firmly rejected, which nonetheless did not stop it from receiving advice and help from both Western powers – particularly Britain, where plans had been made to install a Swedish headquarters in exile for the government and the person who would most likely have served as a civilian "Supreme Commander in exile", Alvar Lindencrona. This national independence was reflected in the resistance organization's name, which was not Stay behind (the first word capitalized) but Metro. The English expression *stay behind* is, rather, a conventional designation for the activity to which the Swedish resistance organization devoted itself for almost five decades – from 1949 until at least the mid-1990s – and across three generations of leaders, namely, to stay behind on occupied territory and in various ways work for its liberation.

---

This history of Sweden's resistance organization is not merely meant to educate the public, but also serves as an instructive analogy and contrast for politicians and other key decision-makers facing present-day problems and conditions.[5] Russia's invasion of Ukraine in 2022 has shown that conventional wars of occupation, contrary to the claims of numerous security policy experts, are not a thing of the past. Its opening battle over the strategic Antonov airport in the town of Hostomel, from which airborne Russian *spetsnaz* forces sought to seize Kiev and abduct or kill the Ukrainian leadership, likewise shows that Cold War invasion scenarios involving a coup-like assault on a national capital remain highly relevant.[6]

Now that European countries in the mid-2020s are once again arming themselves in order to counter threats like these, it is time to consider creating civilian stay-behind structures along the lines of those deployed by Ukraine after Russia's annexation of the Crimean peninsula in 2014.[7] For Sweden, this would mean the country retaining some kind of connection to the old national defence organization, rather than restricting itself to a professionalized, NATO-adapted defence structure in which compulsory military service has stagnated. In which case, some of the methods used by the Swedish resistance organization during the Cold War can be transferred more or less wholesale. For instance, there is an obvious value in having a strictly compartmentalized organization and using basic communication technologies in an era when everyone has a smartphone in their pocket and, knowingly or unknowingly, can easily supply an occupying force with valuable information.[8]

At the same time, circumstances have changed in ways that a successor to the old resistance organization will need to address. In today's decentralized and individualized Sweden, there no longer exist any large popular organizations that might confer legitimacy upon a resistance organization. And because the state's monopoly on various kinds of services has been divided up among a host of profit-driven private companies, there is no longer a single official with sole responsibility, say, for telecommunications, who, like Håkan Sterky, could be assigned a leadership role. That a once formerly homogeneous society has become multi-ethnic, and is now defined by intensely felt differences in religion and social norms and values, likewise further complicates the already challenging task faced by a resistance organization: to promote a collective sense of resistance during an ongoing occupation.[9] Similar divisions are visible in most other European countries.

Clearly, not everything can be modelled on the old resistance organization. In some aspects, it may be wise to make different choices entirely. Whether it was right to keep the organization secret, for example, is very much an open question. As now deceased Supreme Commander Bengt Gustafsson has observed, the knowledge that Sweden – or any state, for that matter – had prepared a resistance organization with the capacity to wreak havoc upon occupying forces could have a deterrent effect on any possible invader.[10] But the Cold War-era resistance organization not only puts these kinds of tactical questions and choices in an interesting new light, it also raises strategic and political questions about how collaboration within NATO – whose latest member is Sweden – ought to work.

## NATIONS FIRST

After decades of presenting itself as an apostle of peace and the world's conscience, Sweden has been forced by Russia's invasion of Ukraine to rediscover the virtues of small-state realism and has pragmatically abandoned its cherished neutrality in favour of NATO membership. Such, at least, is the prevailing narrative. In fact, Sweden's leaders have relapsed into a state of self-sacrificing idealism. The two years that passed between Sweden submitting its membership application in May 2022 and its accession in March 2024 should have made it amply clear that most countries, despite their assurances to the contrary, continue to act according to the logic of the nation state. Finland, for example, did not miss the opportunity to join NATO before Sweden. Yet it could easily have waited before handing over its instrument of ratification to the United States, as a way of showing solidarity with Sweden and repaying its sister nation for support given during the Winter War and the Continuation War, as well as for Sweden's decision to refrain from joining NATO during the Cold War out of consideration for the pressure exerted on Finland by the Soviet Union.[11]

For its part, the United States was not prepared to jeopardize its relationship with Turkey, a geopolitically strategic NATO member, in order to hasten Sweden's membership application. This should hardly be surprising, given that everything the US has and continues to do within NATO, as former diplomat John Bolton has argued, comes down to promoting "hard US national-security interests". Altruism and high-sounding ideals – "warm feelings for Europeans or abstract notions of 'democracy'" – have no place in such an equation.[12]

We Swedes are unwilling to face the truth because we do not understand it. Having abolished all forms of nationalism, not merely in words but also in deeds, we expect others to be similarly committed to cooperation and kindness. Sweden, even before its formal accession, therefore resolved to become NATO's star pupil – to "be NATO", as leading politicians and military commanders put it – and to voluntarily assume whatever functions the country "is given" in the alliance's European defence planning. For the same reason, and to the detriment of its own territorial defence, Sweden is, at the time of writing, planning to deploy considerable military resources beyond its national borders: a battalion in Latvia, as large or larger than Britain's entire Baltic troop contribution; and a whole brigade in northern Finland in the event of a crisis or war.[13]

According to Ulf Kristersson, the country's centre-right Prime Minister since the 2022 election, Sweden can simply "agree with other [NATO countries] that these things do more good elsewhere, given that [their] resources can also be used on our territory".[14] This statement is based on an interpretation of NATO's Article 5 that is widely accepted in Sweden, namely that other members will rush to Sweden's defence if we are attacked while a large portion of our own military forces have been sent somewhere else. Swedes may have taken this idealism and starry-eyed faith further than anyone else, but other Europeans within the alliance are hardly immune. Many member states fail to see NATO for what it is: "a very political alliance", in the words of historian Peter Apps – one that might even be described as an "'organized controversy', attempting to resolve sometimes irreconcilable and enduring differences between its members".[15] In recent years, this tendency has become even more pronounced, with the Secretary General's role evolving from what Javier Solana once called a "catalyst of consensus" into that of frustrated chief whip unsuccessfully trying to control disruptive members.

In this respect, NATO has come to resemble the European Union: a culturally and geographically diverse entity whose members are expected to adhere to the strategic direction set by Brussels and a few major powers, principally the United States. This stands in sharp contrast to the reason for founding

NATO: to counter the global challenge represented by Soviet communism. It is hardly surprising, then, that recent years have seen the emergence of a number of isolationist or anti-NATO political leaders who question the alliance's cohesion and long-term viability. If NATO is to remain relevant, it is in need of reform. And it is here that we can take a page from the Swedish resistance organization during the Cold War.

The men of the resistance organization, we recall, rejected the proposals by the United States and Britain that the stay-behind organization Metro should be placed under their joint control. The Swedes may have feared that if the CIA and MI6 took it over, the resistance organization would cease to be a Swedish defence organization and become instead merely a pawn of the great powers. In this respect, Thede Palm and Chief of the Army Carl August Ehrensvärd, who were the strongest advocates of independence in the resistance organization, were taking a realistic view. Dependence certainly appears to have been the fate of the Norwegian stay-behind organization, to judge from Vilhelm Evang's persistent dissatisfaction with foreign influence.

At the same time, it is fair to say that Palm and Ehrensvärd went too far in their dismissive attitude towards the West, considering the fairly substantial Western aid that the resistance organization would in fact have relied on in the event of an invasion and occupation of Sweden. Indeed, such isolationist thinking among the leadership of the resistance organization shares some features with so-called marginal effect theory, which enjoyed a vogue in defence circles during the 1960s and baselessly presumed that Sweden would only have to confront the marginal numbers of Soviet troops that would be left over in a confrontation with NATO. In this way, the country could "wage its own successful defensive war to protect its territory regardless of how hostilities progressed in the great clash of powers on the continent".[16] In other words, the resistance organization perhaps overestimated its own potential.

There was nothing wrong with their national instincts. On the contrary, they were a strength. But, as always, there is a golden mean. Today's Swedish leaders have made the opposite mistake by neglecting to promote their own country and its sovereignty. Fittingly enough, "NATO first" is the defence doctrine of the newly allied Sweden.[17] Sweden, like other NATO members, must instead strike a judicious balance between improving the prospects of Allied military assistance in the event of an attack and the pursuit of its national interests. Although these goals are not inherently contradictory, NATO's current structure suggests that they have become so.

What if NATO were transformed into an alliance with a more nation-centred character in which the highest degree of military solidarity would only be expected in the event of a threat against all members? Member states would explicitly be allowed to participate in NATO operations around the globe in accordance with how they saw them as aligning with their own national beliefs and interests. If such a rule had been in place during the Ukraine military aid effort, Spain, for example, would not have been reprimanded for focusing on security challenges along its southern border. Under such an arrangement, NATO members would not be required to adhere to a single, often Western-aligned analysis of world affairs but would also remain entitled to collective protection in a World War III-type scenario. Such a doctrine would be in keeping with the realist spirit of the Swedish resistance movement and its counterparts elsewhere in Europe.[18]

## THE LOGIC OF NECESSITY

There is a kind of domestic equivalent to Sweden's habit of following various international resolutions without making an independent national analysis; the phenomenon will be familiar to observers in other countries. I am thinking here of the deep reluctance at all levels of the state to overstep formal authority, an attitude that political scientists James March and Johan Olsen have described – positively – as "the logic of appropriateness".[19] According to this logic, good bureaucratic decision-making proceeds from the issue of what is possible or appropriate in a given situation with regard to the prevailing laws. Individual officials therefore ought not to reflect independently upon whether the rules are identical with the most desirable outcome, but restrict themselves instead to the existing frameworks so as to avoid any danger of challenging the democratically established chain of command.

The "essence of the democratic spirit", as March and Olsen conclude their defence of the logic of appropriateness, is "to try to do good, even while knowing that the efforts may be fruitless or misguided".[20] One-sided and black-and-white thinking of this kind is also what many officials in Sweden and elsewhere regard as democratic public administration, whether they are operative front-line bureaucrats or workers in central agencies and government offices. They seem not to realize that their logic can also be to the detriment of the democratic state and its capacity to protect its citizens and other dependents against different types of threats and social crises. In my view, numerous recent events have highlighted this phenomenon, but let me focus for now on what I see as three particularly illuminating examples.

On a September night in 2024, four unidentified drones violated the airspace above Stockholm's Arlanda airport, resulting in air traffic being suspended for more than two hours. The sabotage was discovered by chance, possibly by passing police officers who saw the drones with the naked eye. Such was the account given by a senior official at the Swedish Civil Aviation Administration, the public body responsible for air traffic in Sweden, in a radio interview the following day. Swedish airports, she explained, in fact lack the technological resources to detect (and disrupt) objects such as drones "that do not have lights on them" and "do not follow the rules" of air safety.[21]

The natural follow-up question – why had Arlanda, Sweden's main airport in a strategic location near Stockholm, not purchased such technology? – was met with palpable indifference. Because the "airport operator [the state-owned company Swedavia] owns the airspace around the airport," explained the official, the Civil Aviation Administration does not concern itself with security above ground level. She added: "[At the Civil Aviation Authority] we comply with the regulations that we are bound to follow, and the airport operator is supposed to meet its responsibilities." In the wake of a deliberate violation of protected airspace by drones that could easily have had far graver consequences than air traffic delays, seemingly the only concrete measure that the Civil Aviation Administration planned to take was to write a report about an "operational deviation" and add it to the other documentation. Rarely has respect for the limits of appropriateness been formulated so revealingly.

Another example occurred during the violent winter storm that struck the southern Swedish region of Skåne in January 2024, when almost a thousand cars were stranded in snowdrifts on the southbound lane of the E22 motorway for over 24 hours. One of these was an ambulance transporting a sick patient. It was discovered in the line of vehicles by an electrician and civil defence volunteer from Denmark, who had plenty of tools in his own car. The man, Nicolai Silverbeerg, told a police patrol on the scene that it would not take him "more than half an hour to saw a gap in the central barrier that would let the ambulance drive away".[22] But the police would not allow it, and the man's girlfriend cautioned him against disregarding them. "You're not in Denmark now," she warned him on the phone.

After more time passed, the police on the E22 changed their minds about getting the ambulance out quickly. Yet they dared not take the decision themselves. "They rang to ask for authorization," claims Silverbeerg, "but were denied." Only after seven hours was the ambulance able to leave the line of vehicles – when the fire brigade arrived and immediately cut a hole in the central barrier. Silverbeerg later told a newspaper that, for him, it is "important to have the attitude: Is there a problem here? Then let's fix it." But as his girlfriend's blunt comments at the time made clear, this time he had run into a *Swedish* problem, which often tends to have no quick or rational solution.

The truth of this maxim is also demonstrated by a third example: Sweden's hesitant evacuation of its local staff from Afghanistan during the final chaotic days of West-friendly rule in August 2021, as exhaustively detailed by author Robert Karjel. At considerable personal risk, hundreds of Afghans had assisted Sweden in various capacities in Afghanistan, including as guards for diplomats and interpreters for Swedish soldiers fighting the Taliban. Sweden had been dependent upon Afghan collaborators during two decades of fruitless nation-building. But when the country completely collapsed and Kabul faced imminent recapture by the Taliban, Stockholm initially considered abandoning these loyal collaborators on the grounds that they were not Sweden's formal responsibility.

The question of moral versus purely legal responsibility had already arisen ten years earlier in connection with the dismantling of Swedish bases in northern Afghanistan. Only reluctantly and after public debate were a handful of interpreters granted Swedish residence permits. "It was a recurring challenge for Sweden," writes Karjel pointedly, "a special case that had been thrown up by events which did not fit into the pre-existing system of laws and rules."[23] Rescuing in real time people who had served Sweden during the Taliban takeover was understandably regarded as an even more sensitive task. Finally, after much indecisiveness, the Ministry of Foreign Affairs and the Swedish Migration Agency pressed for the local staff to be evacuated to Sweden.

But by this point the Swedish Armed Forces had formally concluded its deployment in Afghanistan, and its lawyers refused to guarantee that Swedish soldiers had an armed mandate in what it could now be argued was a country like any other. It therefore fell to Vesper, a Swedish private security company that had been contracted to protect Sweden's embassy in Kabul, to lead the operation, with the tacit approval of the various official agencies, and in practice decide which people should be saved from among an enormous wave of refugees. Such is the absurdity – that the state, on so basic an issue as who is regarded as having the right to relocate to the country, should outsource the exercise of public authority to a private company – that can arise when a bureaucratic culture takes appropriateness as its guiding light.

By comparison, the British government fares rather better. In August 2023, after learning of a data breach in which the identities of tens of thousands of Afghans who supported UK operations in Afghanistan were allegedly exposed to the resurgent Taliban, Defence Secretary Ben Wallace imposed a media blackout by securing a super-injunction on the grounds that there was a threat to life. His successor, Grant Shapps, opted not to brief the opposition or relevant parliamentary committees. Military housing in the UK was repurposed to accommodate Afghan collaborators who might have been compromised. Mistakes were made, certainly. But one can hardly accuse the government of following any "logic of appropriateness". Perhaps it was something else: a logic of necessity.[24]

The Swedish resistance organization during the Cold War was the result and extension of that same logic of necessity. The emblematic example is the pragmatism of its founder, Tage Erlander. There was no clear constitutional basis for the formation of the resistance organization in 1949. And yet it happened. Erlander clearly saw that the letters he had issued in his capacity as Prime Minister were a sufficient makeshift at a time of acute insecurity for Sweden, which was made even more insecure by King Gustaf V's dementia and the impending change of head of state. Only when the situation had stabilized on all fronts did Erlander initiate a government decision that removed any doubts as to the resistance organization's formal legality. In a word, he did what was necessary first and then what was appropriate. It is a principle that the West would do well to revive.

# Afterwords

## ON SOURCES AND METHOD

This book seeks to offer a so-called total history of the Swedish resistance organization during the Cold War. This means that I do not restrict myself to a particular aspect of the phenomenon but gather all strands – political, military, interpersonal and even socio-cultural – into a whole. A different author could doubtless have woven another web; I leave it to the reader to judge the cogency of my arguments.

My approach to the subject is inspired by the German historian Karl Schlögel's magnum opus on the principal scene in the bloodiest period of Joseph Stalin's rule, *Moscow, 1937*. More precisely, Schlögel's methodological line of argument about the "stereoscopic all-round view" that he describes (in characteristically German style) as:

> [B]etter suited to the disparate nature of the world than is a strenuous, concentrated tunnel vision. By taking in everything "at a glance", it grasps the relationships that elude a more specialized but also a more limited mode of perception.[1]

A far-reaching research scope of this kind is well suited to my aim in this study – which, like Schlögel's, seeks to open up rather than close down lines of enquiry – to capture the historical reality in all its complexity and to stimulate more extensive investigations into the various aspects of the Swedish resistance organization.[2] There is, as I observed in the prologue to this book, a lack of primary research in this area.

My own "total" contribution builds on a rich and varied body of source materials that comprise artefacts, written sources and oral narratives from living sources – too many to examine individually. Three key sources nonetheless deserve a more detailed explanation of the condition in which I discovered them and how they advanced my research.

The first of these sources is the work diary that historian Thede Palm kept, virtually every day, for the almost two decades (1946–64) that he was director of the intelligence service T Bureau and for one year thereafter. According to peace and conflict studies scholar Wilhelm Agrell, it is "the most important and most fabled source material in the Swedish intelligence service's modern history".[3] Palm himself claimed to have regularly dictated its contents to his two secretaries, who were meant to be the only people who knew that he was keeping the diary. The names of individuals "which not even these ladies were supposed to know" were dictated in abbreviated form.[4]

The diary's physical appearance indicates that it genuinely dates from the period in question and largely came about in the manner Palm describes. It comprises two subsequently bound volumes of several thousand yellowing and unpaginated sheets of paper that exhibit variations over time in type impression, ribbon colour and line spacing. In both the margins and the body text there are notes in pencil or ballpoint pen, typically of a name. In addition, there are numerous handwritten pages containing diary notes in chronological order, memos, and lengthy summaries of various meetings. All of the entries from the year 1965, by which time Palm had left T Bureau, are written by hand on ruled paper. The diary is preserved in the Swedish Military Archives, where it was sealed, in accordance with Palm's wishes, until 2016. Since then, I and a handful of others have been permitted to read the material for research purposes and subject to so-called confidentiality conditions. Today, the diary is fully declassified.

What no previous researcher into this material seems to have realized, however, is that it includes a description of the formation of the secret resistance organization as seen from Palm's perspective. Even though the diary's narratorial voice is never challenged, as a contemporary document it is, needless to say, an invaluable first-hand source. Among other things, it enabled me to draw up a historical chronology and to map out the organization's secret network of loyal recruits. Wilhelm Agrell, despite relying heavily on the diary, makes no mention of Palm's stay-behind material in his history of the Swedish intelligence service. Although Fredrik von Arnold, first secretary of the Neutrality Policy Commission and later of the Security Services Commission, was given special permission to read Palm's diary while it was still embargoed, in conversation with me he could not remember it having contained anything essential about the resistance organization. The reason for this oversight, if such it is, probably lies in Palm's habit of using code words – often highly enigmatic – in order to protect individuals, locations and groups associated with his various activities.[5]

But since Palm had explicitly stated during his cross-examination by the Neutrality Policy Commission (on which more later) that he had kept a full account of the resistance organization in his diary, I decided to review the material with that particular object in mind. By virtue of having gained access to the personal diaries and letters of resistance leader Alvar Lindencrona and other key figures (including Palm's own correspondence) as well as other secondary materials, I was able – like the enemy spy whom Swedish wartime posters warned about – to "join the dots" and decipher the most important codenames. I was then in a position to read in plain language Palm's account of the resistance organization.

I have been selective in reproducing information from Palm's diary, however, and have excluded details that I feel are overly complicated or technical, such as the countless twists and turns involved in securing suitable radio equipment for the resistance organization. I have also excluded a number of individuals who, although referenced by Palm in relation to the resistance organization, seem to me to be extraneous to our understanding of the stay-behind phenomenon in Sweden.

The second key source for this investigation comprises the transcripts of the Neutrality Policy Commission's cross-examination of practically everyone – government ministers, heads of public bodies, diplomats and military personnel – who played a central role in Sweden's foreign and security policy during the Cold War and was still alive when the commission carried out its inquiry in the early 1990s. In many cases, relatively little time had passed since the informant's period of active service, making their information highly reliable. All of those cross-examined had also been promised (baselessly, as it would turn out) that the transcripts would remain classified in perpetuity. Most of the documents are verbatim transcripts of sound recordings in the form of questions and answers, while a smaller number are fairly loose summaries of what had been said. The documents bear the date of the hearing but in most cases do not record when the transcription or summary was made. The original minutes of the conversations are preserved in the Central Archives of the Government Offices.

By happy coincidence, when I began my research in 2021, the Social Democratic government had just decided to make the hitherto largest release of documents, 104 in total. As a result I was able to immediately request access to these documents that were now in the public domain. (I secured access to certain other research materials that fell outside the scope of the decision, such as a letter to the Commission from former Minister of the Interior Eije Mossberg, by filing a special request.) Information still considered secret was redacted or replaced by blank pages.

A handful of the transcripts contained classified information that, to judge from the context, related to the Swedish resistance organization. I made a request to the following centre-right government to be allowed to read these particular sections, if necessary subject to confidentiality conditions. Regrettably, my request was denied on the grounds of the Public Access to Information and Secrecy Act (OSL).

Despite this decision, the transcripts in the form that I was able to access them provided a surprising amount of highly concrete information about what various decision-makers knew and thought about the resistance organization. The documents also led to other sources – most importantly, Thede Palm's diary – and individuals whom I approached for interviews, such as intelligence officer and public official Ingemar Engman. It is my hope that this unique body of material will one day be released in its entirety to researchers and the general public. In my view, the country's government does not have proprietary rights over historical events that are a matter of concern for all Swedes and whose publication today cannot reasonably be said to be detrimental to Sweden's security. Moreover, regardless of the year in which it was communicated to the members of the Neutrality Policy Commission, much of the information has now exceeded the maximum security classification period of 70 years.

My third key source for this investigation has been the Council decision of 1955 – until 2005 strictly classified – to fully legalize the Swedish resistance organization. My discovery of this decision definitively refutes those who would claim that the Swedish stay-behind organization was an extra-parliamentary configuration. Although, as discussed in Chapter 5, I was not certain that this document actually existed, I had a stroke of luck. The National Archives were unable to locate the decision when I requested a search of the old Ministry of the Interior's so-called secret archive for what I thought (mistakenly, it turned out) was the relevant time period, and I was forced to put the matter to one side. But I was determined to go through the list of potentially relevant archive headings in the register of the secret archive that historian Magnus Hjort compiled during his investigation of the resistance organization in the early 2000s and that he kindly shared with me. So I made my way to the National Archives reading room.

None of the files that Hjort thought might be of general significance and that I ordered up turned out to relate to the resistance organization. But the files were delivered together with other papers, and so I leafed through the folders of documents, bearing in mind the motto of American historian Robert A. Caro: "Turn every page."[6] Suddenly, I had the original Council decision in front of me on the table – three pages together with their original blue-and-yellow document ribbon, royal seal, and the signatures of Gustaf VI Adolf and the minister responsible, Minister of the Interior Gunnar Hedlund. Such is the role that serendipity can sometimes play in research. Naturally there is much truth in the famous observation of French chemist Louis Pasteur that "chance favours the prepared mind", but while working on this book I have also come to believe that scholarly discoveries can, in some unfathomable way, be destined for a particular person. Chance waits, we might say, for the right mind.

Favourable circumstances have also helped me to find many of my interviewees, around 30 in total. For example, after I described my research project in a Swedish radio programme in December 2021, I was contacted by the relatives of resistance organization members, both deceased and still living, whom I would otherwise have had no way of finding.[7] I identified and got in touch with more centrally placed individuals on my own initiative. Although most had never spoken, or at least not as openly, about their knowledge of the resistance organization, they were persuaded by the fact that the enquiry came from a researcher rather than a journalist. I cannot be certain but I also believe that another factor was the climate of anxiety in and around Sweden following Russia's invasion of Ukraine in 2022.

For the centrally placed sources, I conducted what are known as semi-structured interviews, which rely on prepared lists of questions. For the other subjects, including relatives, I listened in a more open fashion to what they had to say while noting to what extent it corresponded with what I had already been able to establish. I returned to several of these sources for informal conversations. Most of the formal interviews lasted an hour or more, and all were recorded. Because the interviews in several cases touched on the decision-maker's views on other interesting issues besides the resistance organization, I hope to be able to preserve them in an archive, where, subject to certain conditions, they can be available to future researchers.

Oral history has an undeservedly poor reputation in social research. Historians of secret services and similar bodies are often forced to rely upon spoken statements, either because the activities in question are undocumented or because the archives that exist are guarded by the authorities.[8] In doing so, however, they are not merely making a virtue out of necessity. In intelligence research, for example, initiatives such as the Belfast Project, which gathered testimony from Northern Irish paramilitary organizations, have shown that writing history on the basis of living sources can be valuable in its own right.[9] My own project, it is true, has been able to draw upon an unusually extensive body of written source materials, but my account would nonetheless have been incomplete without oral testimony.

Total history is predicated on the ambition of describing its subject from all perspectives and angles. For example, how the resistance organization was viewed by its grassroots operatives cannot be established from documents alone. Even so, I have treated all of my oral accounts with an awareness of their limitations as source materials. As far as possible I have tried to corroborate informants' statements about their roles and duties with at least one written source or at least one other (independent) living source. I have deliberately avoided anonymizing my interviewees, with the exception of three instances where I have omitted a surname in order to protect a source, and I have been transparent about who provided the information and when, so that readers can make up their own minds as to its reliability.

In accordance with this principle of transparency, I also invited all of my sources who were still alive at the time of the book's completion to read the quotations from their own testimony. A secondary reason for doing this was that my sources should feel comfortable about, and in some measure be able to influence, how they are presented in the book. In the few instances where we were not in agreement, I have tried to balance their requests with the public interest and scholarly ethics. Such accommodations cannot be offered to the book's historical figures, of course, but even there I have sought to portray them in a way that they would have found acceptable – and perhaps even appreciated.

## THE HUMAN COST – ELISABETH'S STORY

### *"Sweden came first"*

Something that this book has hitherto only indirectly alluded to but that deserves more detailed consideration is the fact that many of the children of active members of stay-behind organizations were used to further various tactical objectives. For example, their unwitting compliance made it possible to arrange meetings in public spaces and other countries or to carry out effective reconnaissance of suitable areas for use in the event of invasion and occupation. In situations like these, it was naturally convenient for a stay-behind operator to be able to divert a suspicious or curious gaze by means of an oblivious or even childish "decoy". While such distraction tactics can sometimes be necessary and defensible from a military point of view, they risk negatively impacting the families involved. Siblings can be made to feel that they are not as close to their parents as the brother or sister who is continually invited to go with them on trips and other activities. And the children being exploited may be forced later in life to recognize that the special attention they received was largely instrumental, prompting a profound re-evaluation of their relationship to their mother or father.

Let us recall, for example, the pitiful remark made by the daughter of A. J., a regional director of the Swedish resistance organization, in a newspaper interview in 1998: "All those Sunday excursions – I thought they were for our sake."[10] Just how deceitful (and potentially dangerous) such parental behaviour can be, even when it has good intentions, is indicated by Johan Giesecke's astonished reply to the question of whether his father Curt-Steffan used any of his children as decoys: "You mean, that we would have been like actors? No, he would never have done that."[11] This was true: Curt-Steffan Giesecke never involved his family in the resistance organization's activities. By his own account, he "never travelled with any kind of 'cover'".[12]

But Alvar Lindencrona, his predecessor as commander, certainly did. Frozen cucumber sandwiches are Elisabeth Lindencrona Paues's strongest memory of the first time she acted as a decoy for her father Alvar. The occasion was a car journey they made together on a wintry country road beside Lake Vättern in an eye-catching car, a chauffeur-driven Mercedes that belonged to the insurance company Thule. As Elisabeth explains:

> I was just a little girl and it was supposed to look like a family excursion. Father had persuaded me by saying that we would have a nice picnic with sandwiches from Thule's restaurant. But he stopped the car in a lay-by along the way and told me that we would eat the picnic there, out of the back of the car. I would have preferred to stay inside but eating in the car was out of the question, and instead I had to be visible on the roadside and eat sandwiches with cucumbers that had frozen on the way, so that all the people could see that Alvar Lindencrona had *his daughter* with him.[13]

This early incident was to establish a pattern in Elisabeth Lindencrona Paues's life.

Outwardly, she was the Lindencrona family's "Duchess", a princess-like figure in the 1940s weekly magazines with her blonde corkscrew curls, ribboned hairband and embroidered dresses.[14] A spirited and cheerful girl who was known in Broms School, where Crown Prince Carl Gustaf later attended primary school, for blithely disregarding the polite forms of address and wanting to be friends with anyone she took a liking to. "'Duchess' may not address me informally but must say 'Mrs Broms'," Elisabeth remembers Anna Broms, the school's owner, sternly instructing her. "Father went into fits of laughter the following day when at school I said: 'Hey, you, Mrs Broms!'" Elisabeth clarifies her relationship with her father: "We belonged together, we were a unit somehow."

In the private world of the family home, however, Elisabeth seems to have had tighter constraints. As she recalled during our first meeting in January 2022: "I was in complete despair about my father's over-protectiveness. We only lived a couple of streets away from Broms School and there were almost no cars in Stockholm in those days, but even so I still wasn't allowed to walk to school by myself."[15] When she got older, Alvar Lindencrona also imposed strict rules on how she was allowed to socialize among her peers: "What boy would want to have the last dance with me, who would always be collected by a chauffeur and could never be walked to the front door for a kiss?"[16] Elisabeth explained that even when an actual princess, Crown Prince Carl Gustaf's older sister Christina, was present, she would be expected to go home first. "I was hopelessly cloistered."[17]

Instead of extending her friendship circle, Elisabeth grew ever closer to her father, who often invited her to come with him on his trips. After her 18th birthday in 1960, these invitations included balls and embassies in foreign capitals, where she invariably found "the red carpet rolled out" for both of them. Alvar Lindencrona's lame explanation for these lavish receptions was that he worked as a kind of roving accountant.[18] On these more festive occasions, Lindencrona saw to it that his daughter was in full view on his arm. Although he encouraged her to mingle, he seems also to have nudged her towards forming connections with the children of ministers and other senior decision-makers. When she was younger, by contrast, Elisabeth made trips within Sweden during which she was sometimes left alone for long periods of time in a hotel room or some out of the way place. On one of these trips, her father took her to the house of the Chief of the Army Carl August Ehrensvärd. "I had to sit on a blanket on grass by the road," says Elisabeth, adding with emotion in her voice: "Father had brought me along for appearances."

On another occasion, Elisabeth was given to believe that she and her father would be going skiing, just the two of them, at Siljansborg in Dalarna County. But as soon as Lindencrona had finished a private dinner with a Swedish diplomat whom Elisabeth knew as a family friend, and who also turned out to be a guest at the ski hotel, he told his daughter that they would have to go home because there was not enough snow.[19] As Elisabeth sees it, the fact that people close to her thought that Alvar Lindencrona treated her as his favourite created an "imbalance in the family". The unbreakable loyalty that she felt – indeed, in some ways still feels – to her father prevented her from telling them how she often felt on those trips. "I never talked about it. I could never say anything negative about Father," she explains. At the same time, she sometimes felt slighted or hurt when it came to getting her father's attention at home. When during her teens she was hospitalized for water in her lungs as a result of Asian flu, he did not come to visit her.

It was thus a hard blow for Elisabeth when in 1981 her father told her, in strictest confidence, that he had had a secret mission during her childhood, implicitly admitting that this had been the real reason why he always wanted to have her accompany him everywhere. "I don't want to sound like a martyr – I accept that Sweden came first for Father," Elisabeth stresses, but adds: "My life would have been completely different if he had not been in the stay-behind organization."[20]

This statement acquires a new and ambiguous significance for Elisabeth after reading a draft of this chapter in March 2025. She explains that my account has helped her to reconcile herself to her childhood and that she now views several of the incidents I describe in a slightly different light. She observes – correctly,

I think – that she also gained something by being a cover for her father. The role enabled her to hone her social skills and knowledge of languages in settings where there were almost no people her age. She also says that she is convinced that Alvar Lindencrona wanted to make it up to his "brave little soldier" in some way when she became an adult, but that he died before getting the opportunity.[21] All the same, Elisabeth insists that she was not entirely free to make her own life choices.

*Through the looking-glass*

For Elisabeth Lindencrona Paues, the single largest decision that a person can be asked to take – whom you choose to share your life with – was affected by her father's deep involvement in the Swedish resistance movement. Such, at least, is her conviction. "Father rushed me into getting married," she says: "He got scared and wanted me to marry earlier than I had planned."[22] But scared of what? In the wake of newspaper revelations in 1990–91 that Sweden had prepared a secret resistance organization, Bjarne Stenquist, a journalist at *Dagens Nyheter*, claimed that the Soviet Union had for decades known "everything about the group".[23] According to Stenquist, one day in the 1960s the "deputy director of MI6" showed up in Stockholm with the message that Donald Prater, the British intelligence service's field officer in Stockholm, "had for several years been working for the KGB". The Swedes concluded that the Swedish resistance organization, which had collaborated with the British, was therefore compromised.

It is this spy affair that Elisabeth suspects was the primary reason why, in February 1965, her father unexpectedly insisted that she should move forward the date of her wedding to her fiancé Staffan Paues, then a student at Sweden's Royal Institute of Technology. Only a year earlier, Lindencrona had told Elisabeth in a letter that she should not rush into marriage but continue living at "her old father's house for many more years" and not let go of her family "until you are quite, quite certain".[24] Now there was suddenly a rush to get Elisabeth out of the family home.

Staffan Paues came from a respected family, was training as a mining engineer – a course largely reserved for the sons of Sweden's elite – and was generally seen as an eligible bachelor. But Elisabeth says that she was still unsure as to whether she was ready to take the leap and get married: "I was in love with Staffan but also felt that I didn't yet really know him. We had never been alone together. I also felt that Staffan's parents were against the match because I had no dowry." Her fiancé, too, wanted at least the summer in which to get to know Elisabeth better, and as a student he did not have the means to support a wife. But Alvar Lindencrona offered to support him financially until he had secured a position, so that the couple could marry as soon as possible. Even though Staffan and Elisabeth dared not refuse, they were both nonetheless scolded by Lindencrona when Elisabeth did not come home for dinner one evening because she and Staffan had been sitting up late writing invitation cards to the wedding. "It was because Father had found out that a spy had been caught and he wanted to protect me from the Russians," speculates Elisabeth, who remembers both her parents being strangely unsettled and anxious about her well-being in late winter that year.[25]

However, if that was the reason, it was unlikely to have been about Donald Prater. According to *Dagens Nyheter*, that spy affair did not take place until 1968, three years after Elisabeth and Staffan got married. Interestingly, not long afterwards the paper withdrew its claims about Prater in an article headlined "Wrong Man Identified". For reasons that were not stated, the editor explained that Prater had neither "any involvement whatsoever with the KGB" nor "known about the Swedish resistance organization that during the 1960s was led by former insurance executive Alvar Lindencrona".[26] However, the newspaper continued to maintain that the resistance organization had been exposed to the Soviet Union.

In a reversal that is typical of the intelligence services' mirror-world, I can confirm that Donald Prater was indeed the suspected traitor. This much is clear from a memo preserved in Thede

Palm's diary and written in May 1970, five years after Palm left the intelligence service T Bureau. Palm seems to have done a service to the subsequent Swedish intelligence organization IB as well as Britain's MI6 by getting in touch with his old contacts in Her Majesty's secret service and discussing the "Prater case" with them. He reports home that Prater has been revealed "to have been a communist in Oxford before the [Second World] War" and also a "secret party member", but that since then there is no "evidence that he has done anything illegal or even had any anomalous contacts outside of his duties". Prater, Palm adds, also conducted himself "exemplarily" during his time in Stockholm.[27] According to Palm, the British would have been grateful for intelligence from Sweden "that could be connected to potentially illegal activity on his [Prater's] part", but the former chief of Swedish intelligence seems not to have had any such information to offer.[28]

This is also my conclusion after reading Palm's diary and correspondence. Prater is hardly mentioned, and when he is, from what I can tell it is never in a stay-behind context. Palm discussed stay-behind operations with other representatives from MI6. Hence, it is unclear whether Prater was a spy at all and, moreover, whether he actually knew anything of real significance about the Swedish resistance organization. The chronicler of British intelligence, Nigel West, has told me in conversation that Prater, because of his political background, may simply have been the victim of one of the sweeping and sometimes arbitrary purges that took place within MI6 following the Kim Philby affair.[29]

Returning to the mirror-world, none of this sheds any light on Alvar Lindencrona's reasons for pressuring his daughter Elisabeth and her fiancé Staffan to get married in 1965. West points out that the so-called Venona traffic of Soviet telegrams that were deciphered by American signals intelligence in the 1940s and 1950s supports the theory that there were a number of active Soviet agents in Sweden with far-reaching connections inside the Swedish establishment.[30] We cannot exclude the possibility, therefore, that Lindencrona had been informed of the existence of another spy who threatened the resistance organization and, ultimately, his own daughter. But nor can we entirely exclude the possibility that he had quite different, private reasons.

Elisabeth will never know for certain to what extent her path in life has been affected by Sweden's secret resistance organization. She is content to believe that her father feared for her life. And this is only one of the many loose threads that the resistance organization has left behind. As Thede Palm reported his British colleagues as concluding about the enigmatic and unresolved Prater affair – "the file is open".[31]

# Acknowledgements

Special thanks to:

Ilija and Sanja Batljan
The Hans and Barbara Bergstrom Foundation
Stiftelsen Clas Groschinskys Minnesfond
Stiftelsen Fritt Näringsliv
Peder Johnson
Anders Lindström
Stiftelsen Mellby Gård
Dan Olofsson
Sven och Dagmar Saléns Stiftelse
Björn och Inger Savéns Stiftelse
Stockholms Köpmansklubb and its former chairperson Dag Klackenberg
Patrik and Anna Tigerschiöld
Annika och Gabriel Urwitz Stiftelse

As well as another sponsor to whom I direct my gratitude more discreetly. Without their generous support I could not have written this book.

I am also indebted to Magnus Henrekson, far-sighted former director of the Research Institute of Industrial Economics (IFN), who helped me to secure funding for the book and for many years gave me a professional home at the Institute, which lies, appropriately, a stone's throw from IB's old foreign section on Grevgatan in Stockholm.

After the Institute came under new management, I relocated to the Swedish Defence University, which has in every possible way been an ideal environment in which to complete my research. I am deeply grateful to Niklas Wikström and Jan Ångström, who arranged my appointment as a research fellow at the Department of War Studies in 2023, and to my colleague and now good friend Magnus Christiansson, who has made me feel at home in the Strategy Division.

I feel honoured to have been able to present my findings to cabinet ministers Carl-Oskar Bohlin, Pål Jonson and Gunnar Strömmer – whose government has released several hitherto classified files from ambassador Rolf Ekeus' Security Policy Inquiry – as well as at seminars convened by the Centre for Statecraft and Strategic Communication at the Stockholm School of Economics, the research group Modern Warfare at the Swedish Defence University, the research group for intelligence analysis at Lund University, the Trade Union Confederation (LO), the Swedish Civil Contingencies Agency (MSB), the Norrland Dragoon Regiment (K4) in Arvidsjaur, the National Archives in Arninge (the War Archives), the Confederation of Swedish Enterprise, and Timbro. The Confederation of Swedish Enterprise has additionally given me unrestricted access to its archive at the Centre for Business History, Bromma.

Bo Berg, now-retired head of the Swedish Military Archives, has likewise made available various personal archives that are, or were until recently, restricted to researchers.

Johan Andersson and Torbjörn Schmidt allowed me to borrow the books I needed from, respectively, the Anna Lindh Library and Sällskapet's unique private collection of biographical materials.

Elisabeth Lindencrona Paues provided me with archival materials about her father Alvar Lindencrona, the insurance company Thule and the port of Grundsund, and put me in contact with three other informants.

Gustaf Lindencrona gave his blessing to my working with Alvar Lindencrona's archive in the National Archives and permitted me to copy the collection of pocket calendars and notebooks belonging to Alvar Lindencrona that are now in Gustaf's private possession.

Andreas von der Heide and Jan Nygren have been ambassadors for the book and opened doors to sources that, in the absence of their help, would likely have remained closed. Erik Belfrage had offered to be of similar service but sadly passed away prematurely during the COVID-19 pandemic in 2020.

Peter Englund very kindly met me at Ofvandahls in Uppsala to discuss how to conduct and present historical research, and to wish me *Hals- und Beinbruch*. Andrew Roberts gave me valuable advice on the same subject, and, of course, wrote the all-too-generous foreword to this edition.

The following have read parts or all of my manuscript: Jan Ångström, Eric Bergelin, Henrik Berggren, Mats Bergstrand, Hans Bergström, Magnus Christiansson, Matthew Ford, David Gebre-Medhin, Andreas von der Heide, Magnus Henrekson, Magnus Hjort, Bengt Jangfeldt, Hanna Jungwallius, Dag Klackenberg, P. M. Nilsson, Björn Nolén, Tua Sandman, Björn von Sydow, Lars Trägårdh, Karl Weigelt, Jacob Westberg, Jerker Widén, Niklas Wikström and Kent Zetterberg. Many of its improvements are due to them; any errors are my own.

Gunnar Karlson, former Chief of the Military Intelligence and Security Service (MUST), has, in his capacity as an unusually knowledgeable private citizen, read the manuscript with a keen eye to any possible risks to key Swedish defence assets.

Magnus Hjort let me take charge of his own research notes on archives that might be worth examining in a stay-behind context. Mikael Holmström was similarly generous in sharing his unedited interviews with Curt-Steffan Giesecke for his book *The Secret Alliance*. Thomas Kanger helped me interpret his interview notes with quotes from Reinhold Geijer.

Magnus Andersson introduced me to the concept of "logic of appropriateness". Carl Cederström provided me with literature on the Thule building. Christer Larsson told me about his radio reports in the 1990s. Björn Nolén sparked my interest in the "homeland stewards" and Anders Grafström's posthumous papers. Daniel Suhonen brought my attention to one of Tage Erlander's letters of authorization. Eric Sundström showed me the areas inside the Trade Union Confederation's headquarters that were once a shooting range and arms store. Tommy Svensson familiarized me with the Employers' Confederation's total defence activities. Thomas Tynander made me aware of Allan Mann. Rickard Wessman and Carl Johan Rundquist taught me about Swedish insurance company history. Jerker Widén discussed, within the constraints of official secrecy, the work of the Security Policy Inquiry.

A number of sources whom I interviewed but whose information for various reasons unfortunately did not make its way into the book, and whom I will refrain from naming here, gave me vital background insights into the political and military circumstances in Sweden during the Cold War period.

Ole Grøn was my guide in Denmark and introduced me to Niels Gyrsting, whose impressive private archive of Danish resistance organizations sadly did not end up forming part of this project.

Abbe Bonnier has been a fearless and unfailingly encouraging publisher of the original Swedish edition, who advised me throughout to write the book properly rather than quickly. Hanna Eriksson has been a wise and attentive editor in the sensitive process of bringing the book to completion. Stephen Donovan has fashioned a masterly translation from the original Swedish, which was then enthusiastically and meticously edited by Osprey's Brianne Bellio and copyeditor Anne Halliday. In the final months of completing this revised and translated edition, I was sustained by the gentle encouragement of Anoushka Jain.

Anders "Lanta" Ricknell has taught me very concretely what it means to prepare oneself for offering resistance.

My father, Erik Wennström, has, as always, been my first reader.

My wife, Malin Hasselblad Wennström, has shown admirable patience with a project that has spanned several years, particularly towards the end when she shouldered many family duties to allow me to concentrate on completing the book. For this, and for her unfailing loyalty, I am deeply grateful. I dedicate the results of long years spent on this project to our boys, August and Ingmar – in the hope that they will never have to experience war in their own country.

Johan Wennström

# Notes

PROLOGUE

1 Interview with Bengt on 16 February 2022. Unless otherwise indicated, quotations are drawn from the same interview session as that cited in the first note of each new chapter in which a quotation appears. The term interview here refers to a (semi-)structured and documented interview, whereas more informal conversations have not been systematically documented.
2 Email reply from Bengt, 27 April 2022. On Allan Mann, see Tynander 2023.
3 "Arméns Dag mitt i Stockholm: 50 000 på första parkett", *Armén och vi*, supplement to *Svenska Dagbladet*, 18 May 1983.
4 Conversation with Curt, 25 January 2022. Conversation, 25 September 2024.
5 Conversation with Olof, 25 September 2024.
6 See, for example, ch. 23 in Jensen 2019.
7 See, for example, Grøn 2018.
8 Conversation with Ole Grøn, 30 March 2022.
9 Neutrality Policy Commission, "Minutes from the meeting with director Ingemar Engman", 16 December 1992. Central Archives of the Government Offices, p. 12.
10 Persson 1990, p. 355.
11 Bjarne Stenquist, "CIA skulle stödja Sverige vid krig", *Dagens Nyheter*, 18 December 1990.
12 Interview with Fredrik von Arnold, 17 January 2023.

13 Neutrality Policy Commission, "Tape recordings from 'Dagens Eko' and 'Kanalen' concerning information on Swedish wartime coordination with NATO". Central Archives of the Government Offices, p. 16.
14 Lars-Olof Lampers, *Det grå brödraskapet: en berättelse om IB*. Report to the Security Services Commission, SOU 2002:92, p. 467.
15 Bjarne Stenquist, "Hemlig grupp aktiv ännu", *Dagens Nyheter*, 14 August 1991.
16 "Kalla Fakta", TV4, 21 April 1996. See also Annika Carlsson, "Motståndsmän träder fram", *Svenska Dagbladet*, 22 April 1996.
17 Thomas Kanger and Oscar Hedin, "Erlanders hemliga gerilla", *Dagens Nyheter*, 4 October 1998.
18 Forsberg and Christiansson 2025, pp. 58–59. (Italics in original.)
19 Holmström 2011, pp. 389–418.
20 Ulf Eliasson and Magnus Hjort, "Det kalla kriget i personarkivens spegel", *Arkiv, samhälle och forskning* no. 1 1999.
21 Holmström 2011, p. 391.
22 Security Policy Inquiry, *Fred och säkerhet*, SOU 2002:108, part 2. Fritzes 2002, p. 750. (I have italicized *Stay behind*.) Rolf Ekeus met Curt-Steffan Giesecke on 25 April 2002. Security Policy Inquiry, "Minutes from the meeting with Curt-Steffan Giesecke", 26 April 2002, Central Archives of the Government Offices. The inquiry further noted that the resistance movement was still regarded as sensitive within the government in 2002, which contradicts the portrayal of the resistance movement as irrelevant after 1969. Security Policy Inquiry, "Internal memorandum concerning stay behind", 30 October 2002, Central Archives of the Government Offices. Secrecy lifted by administrative decision on 27 May 2025.
23 Eliasson and Hjort 1999; Magnus Hjort, "1949 – An Embryo of an Underground Resistance Movement Takes Shape", unpublished conference paper, 2005. https://www.academia.edu/85034040/1949_An_embryo_of_an_Underground_Resistance_Movement_takes_shape
24 See, for example, Zetterberg 2021a.
25 For a critical assessment, see, for example, Peer Henrik Hansen, "Falling Flat on the Stay-Behinds", *International Journal of Intelligence* 19 (1) 2006; Olav Riste, review of Ganser in *Intelligence*

*and National Security* 20 (3) 2005; "'Stay Behind': A Clandestine Cold War Phenomenon", *Journal of Cold War Studies* 16 (4) 2014.

26 Ganser and Deland 2016.

27 Santesson 2024, p. 342.

28 "Kalla Fakta", TV4, 21 April 1996.

29 Leopold Nuti and Olav Riste, "Introduction: Strategy of 'Stay-Behind'," *Journal of Strategic Studies* 30 (6) 2007, p. 933. On Norway and Denmark, see references throughout this book. On Holland, see Dick Engelen, "Lessons Learned: The Dutch 'Stay-Behind' Organization 1945–1992", *Journal of Strategic Studies* 30 (6) 2007. On West Germany, see Tobias Schmitt, "US Intelligence and the Nascent Transatlantic Security Architecture of the Cold War – the Case of the 'Gesellschaft für Wehrkunde'", *Journal of Intelligence History* 19 (1) 2020. On Switzerland, see Kevin D. Stringer, "Building a Stay-Behind Resistance Organization: The Case of Cold War Switzerland Against the Soviet Union", *Joint Force Quarterly* 85 2017. On France, see Charles Cogan, "'Stay-Behind' in France: Much Ado About Nothing?", *Journal of Strategic Studies* 30 (6) 2007.

30 Francesco Cacciatore, "Stay-Behind Networks and Interim Flexible Strategy: The 'Gladio' Case and US Covert Intervention in Italy in the Cold War", *Intelligence and National Security* 36 (5) 2021, p. 654; Leopoldo Nuti, "The Italian Stay-Behind Network – the Origins of Operation 'Gladio'", *Journal of Strategic Studies* 30 (6) 2007.

31 Zetterberg 2021, p. 276.

32 Daniel Olsson, "Sverige skänkte bort sina fältsjukhus", *Expressen*, 4 April 2020.

33 House of Commons Public Accounts Committee, "Covid-19: Supply of Ventilators", Twenty-Seventh Report of Session 2019–21, p. 3. https://committees.parliament.uk/publications/3639/documents/35370/default/

## CHAPTER 1: A POSSIBLE SCENARIO

1 Winter 1988.

2 See Bo Hugemark, "Berättelsen om *Operation Garbo*", Timbro Medieinstitut 2009.

3 Holmström 2011, p. 16.
4 Gustafsson 2006, p. 48.
5 Interview with Michael Sahlin, 17 November 2022.
6 Bergstrand 2002, p. 127.
7 Hjulström 2017.
8 Gustafsson 2007, p. 62.
9 von Braun and Gyllenhaal 2013, pp. 105–06.
10 Hjulström 2017, pp. 86–87. According to Hugemark 2024, p. 193, the army played down the risks of a surprise scenario because it "was seen as a way to promote the 'blue' branches of the armed forces, that is, the Air Force and the Navy, at the expense of the Army."
11 Interview with Eric Krönmark, 9 February 2022.
12 Interview with Jan Leijonhielm, 14 March 2023.
13 Jansson 2014, p. 174.
14 Jansson 2014, p. 180.
15 Jansson 2023, p. 130. (In the quotation I have italicized *spetsnaz* and expanded an abbreviation.)
16 De Geer 2024, p. 26.
17 Security Policy Inquiry, "Conversation with Admiral Per Rudberg", 9 May 2001. Central Archives of the Government Offices, p. 1. Declassified by governmental decree on 27 March 2024. (In the quotation I have corrected a spelling error.)
18 Michael Sahlin, "Ubåtskrisen på 80-talet", *Kungl. Krigsvetenskapsakademiens Handlingar och Tidskrift* 2012 no. 2, p. 117.
19 Ubåtsskyddskommissionen, *Att möta ubåtshotet,* SOU 1983:13, p. 62.
20 On the Soviet leadership's alarmist worldview, see, for example, Gustafsson 2007 and Jansson 2014.
21 Security Policy Inquiry, "Conversation with Gunnar Nordbeck, Mariefred", 9 September 2002. Central Archives of the Government Offices, p. 5. Declassified by governmental decree on 28 September 2023.
22 Agrell 2000, p. 160.
23 Conversation with Lars-Olov Johansson, 7 May 2024.
24 Conversation with Hanna Jungwallius, 20 March 2024.
25 Blaadh 2025, p. 116.

26 Appendix 2 of "ÖB rapport över ubåtsskyddsverksamheten i Karlskrona-området under februari–april 1984 (4 bilagor)". Edited public-access version. Swedish Defence University Archives, p. 38.
27 Agrell 2000, p. 235.
28 Agrell 2000, p. 241.
29 De Geer 2024, p. 226–27.

## CHAPTER 2: SOMETHING MUST BE DONE

1 Agrell 2017, p. 52.
2 On the West's naivety with regard to Stalin's intentions, see, for example, Petraeus and Roberts 2023, ch. 1.
3 Interview with Ingvar Carlsson, 24 November 2021.
4 Rudberg 1949, p. 199. (In the quotation I have excised the word "But".)
5 Fredholm 2021, pp. 38–45.
6 Fredholm 2021, pp. 42–43.
7 Erlander 2001a, 23 January 1947, pp. 160–61.
8 Fredholm 2021. See also Staffan Bruun, "Finlands mörka dag", *Hufvudstadsbladet*, 20 February 2018.
9 Erlander 2001a, 10 March 1948, p. 211.
10 Erlander 2001a, 18 June 1948, p. 239.
11 Lindbeck 2012, p. 24.
12 Bokholm 2001, p. 161.
13 Jackson 1990, p. 145.
14 Berggren 2022, p. 107.
15 Johansson 2018, p. 69.
16 Carlos Adlercreutz, "1940–1941: G[ränsbyråns] uppgifter", undated notes in pencil. Carlos Adlercreutz's archive, vol. 28. Swedish Military Archives, p. 2. Previously quoted in Rune Svensson, "Sveriges hemliga vapen? C-byråns verksamhet under andra världskriget – en analys av mål, medel, organisation och verksamhet i stort", *Militärhistorisk Tidskrift* 1999.
17 The term is used in "Utkast till plan för Centralbyråns framtida arbetsuppgifter och organisation", Memo 23 May 1945. Defence Staff C Bureau, vol. B 2:5. Swedish Military Archives, p. 1.

18 Hardi-Kovacs 2022, p. 177.
19 Hardi-Kovacs 2022, p. 178.
20 Hardi-Kovacs 2022, p. 178.
21 Rune Svensson, "Sveriges hemliga vapen? C-byråns verksamhet under andra världskriget – en analys av mål, medel, organisation och verksamhet i stort", *Militärhistorisk Tidskrift* 1999, p. 125, n. 78.
22 Carlos Adlercreutz, "1940–1941: G[ränsbyråns] uppgifter", undated notes in pencil. Carlos Adlercreutz's archive, vol. 28. Swedish Military Archives.
23 Berggren 2023, p. 34.
24 Jackson 1990, p. 145.
25 "Svensk lösen", *Dagens Nyheter*, 19 January 1943. Previously quoted in Berggren 2023, p. 30.
26 Bokholm 2001, p. 162.
27 Torsten Nothin, "Några synpunkter på försvarsfrågan", 16 May 1947. Tage Erlander's archive, series E II, vol. 6. Swedish Labour Movement's Archives and Library, p. 4.
28 Erlander 2001a, 1 June 1949, p. 360.
29 Holmström 2011, p. 386.
30 Fredholm 2021, p. 21.
31 Kokk 2001, p. 82.
32 Thomas Lindroth, "Sträng tänkt som motståndsman", *Svenska Dagbladet*, 13 October 1992.
33 Johansson 2018, p. 70.
34 Ulf Eliasson and Magnus Hjort, "Det kalla kriget i personarkivens spegel", *Arkiv, samhälle och forskning* no. 1 1999, p. 17.
35 Thede Palm's diary, 2 June 1949. Thede Palm's archive, vol. 9. Swedish Military Archives, unpaginated. Fully declassified, date not registered. Hereafter cited as Thede Palm's diary and volume.
36 "Total översyn av försvaret, säger Nothin", *Dagens Nyheter*, 7 May 1949.
37 Helge Jung's diary, 25 April 1949. Helge Jung's archive, series B II, vol. 21. Swedish Military Archives, unpaginated. Henceforth Helge Jung's diary and volume.
38 Eliasson and Hjort 1999, p. 17.

39 Helge Jung's diary, vol. 21, 31 May 1949. Previously quoted in Eliasson and Hjort 1999, p. 17.
40 Thede Palm's diary, vol. 9, 15 March 1949.

## CHAPTER 3: THE TOP BRASS

1 Interview with Björn von Sydow, 19 April 2023.
2 See Ruin 1986, pp. 72–77.
3 Erlander 2001a, 12 January 1946, p. 63.
4 Erlander 2001a, 29 December 1949, p. 441.
5 Erlander 2001b, 13 January 1950, p. 17.
6 Erlander 2001a, 19 October 1946, p. 144.
7 Sarotte 2021, p. 23.
8 Erlander 2001b, 8 September 1950, pp. 132–33.
9 After State Council meetings, the ministers usually drank coffee at a café in Stockholm's Old Town, where they were sometimes joined by the Prime Minister.
10 Hans Hederberg, "Den personliga kungamakten varade in på 60-talet", *Dagens Nyheter*, 21 March 1993.
11 On relations between Tage Erlander and Gustaf VI Adolf, see Ruin 1986, pp. 246–54.
12 Thede Palm's diary, vol. 9, 15 November 1950.
13 Neutrality Policy Commission, "Transcript of the questioning of the former Director of Research Thede Palm", 25 February 1993. Central Archives of the Government Offices, p. 23.
14 Thede Palm's diary, vol. 9, 5 December 1949.
15 Alvar Lindencrona's letter of authorization is mentioned in Magnus Hjort, "1949 – An Embryo of an Underground Resistance Movement Takes Shape", unpublished conference paper 2005, p. 3; Carl August Ehrensvärd's letter of authorization has previously been quoted in Ulf Eliasson and Magnus Hjort, "Det kalla kriget i personarkivens spegel", *Arkiv, samhälle och forskning* no. 1 1999, p. 18; Håkan Sterky's letter of authorization is given in facsimile in Erlander 2001a, p. 360; Daniel Suhonen brought to my attention the existence of Anders E. Bjelle's letter of authorization.
16 Letter from Eije Mossberg to the Neutrality Policy Commission, 20 April 1993. Central Archives of the Government Offices, p. 9.

17 Letter to Anders E. Bjelle, Carl August Ehrensvärd and Håkan Sterky, 20 June 1949. Tage Erlander's archive, series 3. Swedish Labour Movement's Archives and Library.
18 Ulf Eliasson and Magnus Hjort, "Det kalla kriget i personarkivens spegel", *Arkiv, samhälle och forskning* no. 1 1999, p. 17.
19 Thede Palm's diary, vol. 9, 5 November 1949. See also the note for 9 November 1949.
20 Helge Jung's diary, vol. 21, 19 September 1949.
21 Thede Palm's diary, vol. 9, 22 June and 2 November 1950.
22 Letter to Carl Eric Almgren, 1 June 1966. Carl Eric Almgren's archive, vol. 01:47. Swedish Military Archives.
23 Thede Palm's diary, vol. 9, 10 December 1949.
24 Letter from Tage Erlander to Alvar Lindencrona, 20 June 1949 with Olof Palme's signature dated 30 June 1970. Archives of the Security Services Commission, Skh vol. 4. Swedish National Archives. Released on 22 November 2023 without restrictions relating to defence secrecy. Magnus Hjort brought to my attention the likely location of this letter of authorization.
25 Thede Palm's diary, vol. 9, 6 December 1949.
26 An incomplete set of pocket calendars belonging to Alvar Lindencrona from the period 1948–67 is preserved in Gustaf Lindencrona's private archive. Copies in the author's archive.
27 Letter to Carl August Ehrensvärd, 12 March 1963. Anders Grafström's archive, vol. 5. Swedish Military Archives.
28 Interview with Elisabeth Lindencrona Paues, 6 January 2022.
29 Interview with Gustaf Lindencrona, 27 October 2021.
30 Rolf af Klintberg, "Vidsträckta kraftinsatser för samhälle och näringsliv", *Svenska Dagbladet*, 15 December 1981.
31 Olof Palme, "Anförande vid Svenska försäkringsföreningens 100-årsjubileum i Gamla Riksdagshuset", 27 February 1975. Olof Palme's archive, vol. 2.4. 0:063. Swedish Labour Movement's Archives and Library, p. 14. On the Palme family's role in the Thule insurance company, see, for example, Berggren 2010, pp. 21–31.
32 The information that Raoul Wallenberg was inspired by the "Scarlet Pimpernel" – or, more precisely, its updated film incarnation in *"Pimpernel" Smith* (1941) – is also noted in Jangfeldt 2012, p. 231.

33 For further references, see, for example, Bernt Bernholm, "Alvar Lindencrona", *Vecko-Journalen* no. 13 1948.
34 "Absolut samtal", SVT, 7 April 1991.
35 Carl Cederström, "Är kontorsråttan på väg tillbaka?", *Svenska Dagbladet*, 5 June 2022. See also Rosell 1981.
36 Grundborn 2006.
37 "Thuleskolan 10 år, idel goda resultat", *Svenska Dagbladet*, 1 June 1957.
38 Grundborn 2006. On Läkarhuset, see also "Läkarcentral vid Odenplan 1964", *Svenska Dagbladet*, 26 October 1961.
39 Quoted in "Politiska fronten", *Svenska Dagbladet*, 11 April 1947.
40 Grundborn 2006, p. 16.
41 Thede Palm's diary, 20 July 1961. Thede Palm's arkiv, vol. 10. Swedish Military Archives, no pagination. Personal confidentiality clause. Henceforth Thede Palm's diary and volume.
42 Letter to dispatcher P. G. Hasselrot, 20 February 1974. Alvar Lindencrona's archive, vol. 1. Swedish National Archives.
43 Letter to Brita Ekdahl, 18 July 1974. Alvar Lindencrona's archive, vol. 1. Swedish National Archives, p. 1. (In the quotation I have changed the word "mine" to "his".)
44 Carl Eric Almgren, "En äkta försvarsvän", *Svenska Dagbladet*, 5 December 1981.
45 The document register of the Swedish National Archives lacks both an acquisition date for the document and information about its provenance. E-mail from Jessica Andersson, 14 May 2024.
46 Ole Grøn and Michael H. Clemmesen, "Skyggerne på væggen: Et forsøg på delvis rekonstruktion af efterretningstjenesten i og fra Sønderjylland fra 1920 til ca. 1950", *Dansk Militærhistorisk Kommissions Tidsskrift* no. 1 2014, p. 93.
47 Conversation with Ole Grøn, 30 March 2022.
48 On Elisabeth Lindencrona Paues, see Afterwords, "The human cost – Elisabeth's story".
49 Letter to managing director Johan Paues, 4 December 1973. Alvar Lindencrona's archive, vol. 1. Swedish National Archives, p. 1.
50 Interview with Ingrid Rosander, 11 January 2022.
51 Vinge 1988, p. 44.

52 Interview with Ingemar Engman, 4 March 2022.
53 The statement is confirmed by Ronald Bye, former party secretary of the Norwegian Labour Party, who stated to the Security Policy Inquiry that "Both Norway and Sweden had secure headquarters in Great Britain, not jointly but as separate facilities." Security Policy Inquiry, "Conversations in Oslo", 22 May 2002. Central Archives of the Government Offices, p. 2. Declassified by governmental decree, 1 August 2024.
54 Mikael Holmström, interview with Curt-Steffan Giesecke, 27 August 2010. Copy in the author's archive.
55 Holmström 2011, p. 415.
56 Interview with Carl Kleman, 22 November 2023. Conversation, 29 November 2023. Conversation, 26 September 2024. Conversation, 11 October 2024.
57 On *Adelsfanan*, see Holmström 2011, p. 405.
58 Conversation with Carl Banér, 11 January 2024. Conversation, 30 September 2024.
59 Åke Hasselrot och Bengt Lännergren, "Ockupation", *Kungl. Krigsvetenskapsakademiens Handlingar och Tidskrift* 1982.
60 Neutrality Policy Commission, "Notes from conversation with former Chief Superintendent Åke Hasselrot", 26 March 1993. Central Archives of the Government Offices, p. 1.
61 Åke Hasselrot and Bengt Lännergren, "Ockupation", *Kungl. Krigsvetenskapsakademiens Handlingar och Tidskrift* 1982, p. 15.
62 Åke Hasselrot and Bengt Lännergren, "Ockupation", *Kungl. Krigsvetenskapsakademiens Handlingar och Tidskrift* 1982, p. 33.
63 Försvarsdepartementet 2021, pp. 36–37.
64 Holmström 2011, p. 41.
65 "PM angående subventionerat civilflyg för att tillgodose militära behov av flygtransporter mm inom landet i krig", 1 December 1951. Nils Swedlund's archive, vol. 6. Swedish Military Archives, p. 1.
66 Evert Taube, "Västkustens största fiskehamn", *Svenska Dagbladet*, 21 July 1918.
67 Grundborn 2012, p. 231.
68 Grundborn 2012, p. 233. On Lars Carlsson, see "Dödsfall", *Dagens Nyheter*, 17 September 1965.
69 The telephone conversation is recorded in an undated handwritten note by Lennart Grundborn, discovered in a copy

of Grundborn's book *Havet vi ärvde* dedicated to Elisabeth Lindencrona Paues. Copy in the author's archive.

70 Alvar Lindencrona, "Försvarets regionala och lokala fastighetsförvaltning", 1 December 1953. Alvar Lindencrona's archive, vol. 5. Swedish National Archives, p. 3.

71 Carl Eric Almgren, "Plan för besök vid I. milbefstaben, F5 och BK 9/11 och 10/11 1953". Alvar Lindencrona's archive, vol. 5. Swedish National Archives, p. 1.

72 This section draws on the author's article "Den demokratiske aristokraten", *Arte et Marte* no. 1 2023.

73 Conversation with Elisabeth Lindencrona Paues, 11 April 2023.

74 Helge Jung's diary, vol. 21, 23 November 1949.

75 Helge Jung's diary, vol. 21, 31 May 1949; first quoted by Ulf Eliasson and Magnus Hjort, "Det kalla kriget i personarkivens spegel", *Arkiv, samhälle och forskning* no. 1 1999, p. 17. See also Helge Jung's diary, vol. 21, 2 June 1949.

76 Erlander 2001b, 8 February 1951, p. 227.

77 Anders Grafström, "C A Ehrensvärd". Manuskript, 27 March 1971. Anders Grafström's archive, vol. 5. Swedish Military Archives, p. 2.

78 Helge Jung's diary, vol. 21, 12 October 1949.

79 Helge Jung's diary, vol. 21, 13 July 1949. See also 9 August 1949.

80 Bergelin 2023, p. 104.

81 Tony Hagström, "Håkan Sterky till minne: automatiserade svenska telenätet", *Svenska Dagbladet*, 29 November 1992.

82 Helge Jung's diary, vol. 25, 16 January 1951.

83 Erlander 2001b, 16 April 1951, p. 262.

84 On the Kempe brothers, see, for example, "Erik Kempe död", *Svenska Dagbladet,* 17 June 1959; "Femton familjer dominerar i näringslivet", *Dagens Nyheter,* 15 February 1968; "Ragnar Kempe: ledande gestalt inom svensk industri", *Svenska Dagbladet,* 13 July 1979. On Carl Kempe, see, for example, Gunnar Unger, "Carl Kempe död", *Svenska Dagbladet*, 9 July 1967.

85 Interview with Bertil Jonsson, 3 October 2022.

86 Erlander 2004, 10 June 1954, p. 88.

87 Arne Geijer's pocket calendar 1954, 10 June. Arne Geijer's archive, vol. 6. Swedish Labour Movement's Archives and Library.

88 Thede Palm's diary, vol. 9, 10 June 1954. (In the quotation I have corrected a punctuation error and the misspelling of a name.)
89 Kassman 1989, p. 69. (Original emphasis.)
90 Kassman 1989, p. 245.
91 Kassman 1989, p. 251.
92 Kassman 1989, p. 136.
93 Interview with Svante Nycander, 23 January 2023.
94 Hansson 1935, pp. 248–49.
95 Torstendahl 1969, p. 164.
96 On the collaboration between the Social Democrats and the Farmers' League, see Ruin 1986, pp. 87–99.
97 See Westerberg 2020, pp. 120–22. See also Lewin 1967, pp. 358–61.
98 Osterman 1973, p. 92.
99 See Husén 1942.
100 Neutrality Policy Commission, "Transcript of the questioning of former Director of Research Thede Palm", 25 February 1993, p. 23.
101 See, for example, Thede Palm's diary, vol. 10, 8 September 1959. See also Civilförsvarsstyrelsen 1961, p. 48.
102 Osterman 1973, p. 238.
103 Swenson 2002, p. 83.
104 Ulf Eliasson and Magnus Hjort, "Det kalla kriget i personarkivens spegel", *Arkiv, samhälle och forskning* no. 1 1999, p. 17.
105 Hjort 1998, p. 21.
106 Thede Palm's diary, vol. 10, 9 December 1961.
107 Thede Palm's diary, vol. 10, 9 January 1962. (In the quotation I have corrected a misspelling of Alvar Lindencrona's name.)
108 Alvar Lindencrona's 1961 pocket calendar, 9 January 1962. Copy in the author's archive.
109 Bertil Kugelberg's desk diary, 9 January 1962. Bertil Kugelberg's papers, SAF archive, series F 51 BH, vol. 3. Centre for Business History.
110 Arne Geijer's 1962 pocket calendar, 8 January. Arne Geijer's archive, vol. 6. Swedish Labour Movement's Archives and Library.
111 Helge Jung's diary, vol. 21, 2 June 1949.
112 On Norgehjälpen, see Kugelberg 1985, pp. 214–69.

113 Letter from Thede Palm, 1 June 1966. Carl Eric Almgren's archive, vol. 01:47. Swedish Military Archives.
114 Mikael Holmström, interview with Curt-Steffan Giesecke, 31 July 2010. Copy in the author's archive.
115 Kugelberg 1986, p. 274. On his successor Curt-Steffan Giesecke, see "Mjukt tronskifte i SAF-borgen", *Svenska Dagbladet*, 25 May 1966.
116 Rothstein 1992, p. 12. (Original emphasis.)
117 Rothstein 1992, p. 173.
118 Kungl. Maj:ts proposition no. 239 (prop. 1947:239), "Angående inrättande av en arbetsmarknadsstyrelse samt förstatligande av den offentliga arbetsförmedlingen m. m." Sveriges riksdag, p. 39.
119 Palm 1988, pp. 84–94.
120 Interview with Göran Tunhammar, 4 November 2022.
121 Lars-Olof Lampers, *Det grå brödraskapet: en berättelse om IB*. Report to the Security Services Commission, SOU 2002:92, p. 466. The otherwise classified record of the Security Services Commission's examination of Curt-Steffan Giesecke contains "very little [...] and nothing of any real detail" about the resistance organization, according to Jessica Andersson, archivist at the Swedish National Archives. Email reply, 25 August 2022. This was verbally confirmed by the Security Services Commission's principal secretary, Fredrik von Arnold, in an interview, 17 January 2023.
122 Interview with Björn von Sydow, 14 December 2021.

## CHAPTER 4: THE OPERATIVES

1 Interview with Fredrik von Arnold, 17 January 2023.
2 Le Carré 1999 [1974], p. 32.
3 Interview with Evabritta Wallberg, 10 January 2023.
4 See Thede Palm, *Wendische Kultstätten: quellenkritische Untersuchungen zu den letzten Jahrhunderten slavischen Heidentums*. Gleerupska universitetsbokhandeln 1937; "Uppsalalunden och Uppsalatemplet", in *Årsbok*. Vetenskapssocieteten i Lund 1942; *Trädkult*. Gleerup 1948.
5 Interview with Jan Leijonhielm, 14 March 2023.

6 Nils Swedlund, "PM angående 'Utredning angående vissa förhållanden vid försvarsstabens numera avvecklande s.k. C-byrå'", June 1948. Nils Swedlund's archive, vol. 6. Swedish Military Archives.
7 Quoted in Rune Svensson, "Sveriges hemliga vapen? C-byråns verksamhet under andra världskriget – en analys av mål, medel, organisation och verksamhet i stort", *Militärhistorisk Tidskrift* 1999, p. 87.
8 Thede Palm's diary, vol. 9, 6 August 1945.
9 Palm 2007, p. 37. On Vilhelm Evang and Norway's stay-behind organization, see Olav Riste and Arnfinn Moland, *"Strengt hemmelig": norsk etterretningsteneste 1945–1970*. Universitetsforlaget 1997. See also Høiland and Bjaaland, vols 1 and 2, 2023 and 2024.
10 Svensson 1999, p. 90. See also Palm 2007, pp. 39–41.
11 Ehrensvärd 2005, 23 January 1946, p. 285.
12 Ehrensvärd 2005, p. 285.
13 Interview with Ebba Palm-Lamoureux, 16 November 2022.
14 Leif Carlsson, "Tycker om galen general", *Svenska Dagbladet*, 28 September 1987.
15 Letter to Sven Andersson, 14 November 1964. Thede Palm's archive, vol. 6. Swedish Military Archives. Personal permission to read restricted material.
16 Hjalmar Gullberg, "Att känna sig själv. En pjäs i tre akter av Thede Palm. 60 sid." 6 June 1950. See also letter from Ragnar Josephson, 20 June 1950. Thede Palm's archive, vol. 2.
17 Between 1946 and 1956, the number of employees at T Bureau doubled to 16, of whom nine (including Palm) had "more qualified duties". See Wikström 2006, p. 68.
18 Fredholm 2021, p. 74.
19 See Thede Palm's archive, vols 1–8, partly restricted.
20 Thede Palm's diary, vol. 9, 1 October 1948. (In this quotation I have changed the word "they" to "we".)
21 Colby and Forbath 1978, pp. 95–96.
22 Thede Palm's diary, vol. 10, 26 June 1963.
23 The incident is examined in passing in Agrell 2017, pp. 163–164.
24 Letter to Dick Helms, 22 October 1962. Thede Palm's archive, vol. 5.

25 Thede Palm's diary, vol. 10, 10 November 1963. (I have shortened the quotation.)
26 Thede Palm's diary, vol. 10, 6 November 1963.
27 Thede Palm's diary, vol. 10, 6 November 1962.
28 Thede Palm's diary, vol. 10, 10 January 1963. (In this quotation I have changed the word "their" to "the CIA's".)
29 Thede Palm's diary, vol. 10, 23 October 1962.
30 Thede Palm's diary, vol. 10, 25 October 1962. (I have adjusted the punctuation in the quotation.)
31 Email from Michael Dobbs, 28 February 2024.
32 See Dobbs 2008, ch. 4.
33 Thede Palm's diary, vol. 10, 6 November 1962.
34 See Zubok and Pleshakov 1996, ch. 7 and 8.
35 Dobbs 2008, pp. 155–58.
36 Thede Palm's diary, vol. 10, 6 November 1962.
37 Thede Palm's diary, vol. 10, 27 December 1964.
38 Thede Palm's diary, vol. 9, 29 May 1952.
39 Thede Palm's diary, vol. 10, 14 May 1963.
40 Thede Palm's diary, vol. 10, 12 November 1964.
41 Conversation with Jan Guillou, 26 March 2024.
42 See, for example, Agrell 2017, ch. 12, and Evabritta Wallberg's introduction to Palm 2007.
43 Interview with Ingemar Engman, 4 March 2022. On Birger Elmér, see Hans Axel Holm, "Första intervjun: så blev jag IB-chef", *Dagens Nyheter*, 8 December 1973.
44 Le Carré 1999, p. 370.
45 Thede Palm's diary, vol. 9, 17 October 1949. See also Neutrality Policy Commission, "Transcript of the questioning of the former Director of Research Thede Palm", 25 February 1993, p. 20.
46 Thede Palm's diary, vol. 9, 11 July 1949.
47 Thede Palm's diary, vol. 9, 5 November 1949.
48 Letter from Thede Palm, 1 June 1966. Carl Eric Almgren's archive, vol. 01:47. Swedish Military Archives. See also Riste 2014, p. 49.
49 Palm 1988, pp. 37, 41.
50 Letter to Alvar Lindencrona, 14 November 1964. Thede Palm's archive, vol. 6.

51 Thede Palm's diary, vol. 10, 24 June 1965.
52 Daily memo, 9 August 1965. Carl Eric Almgren's archive, vol. 01:40. Swedish Military Archives, p. 6. Volume declassified 21 February 2024.
53 Neutrality Policy Commission, "Transcript of the questioning of the former Director of Research Thede Palm", 25 February 1993, pp. 24–25.
54 Neutrality Policy Commission, "Transcript of the questioning of the former Director of Research Thede Palm", 25 February 1993, p. 29.
55 Thede Palm's diary, vol. 10, 10 October 1958.
56 Thede Palm's diary, vol. 10, 29 January 1963. On Alvar Lindencrona's role in diplomatic efforts to create a Swedish affiliation to the European Common Market, see Axel Waldemarson, "Erlanders hemliga mission till de Gaulle", *Svenska Dagbladet*, 15 March 1981.
57 Palm 2007, p. 106.
58 Thede Palm's diary, vol. 10, 20 April 1965. The CIA's new director was William Raborn.
59 Thede Palm's diary, vol. 9, 8 December 1949.
60 Thede Palm's diary, vol. 10, "Memo", 25 June 1964.
61 Neutrality Policy Commission, "Transcript of the questioning of the former Director of Research Thede Palm", 25 February 1993, p. 24.
62 On Elov Bergkvist, see Lars-Erik Falk, "Dödsfall Elov Bergkvist", *Svenska Dagbladet*, 28 June 1999; "Utnämningar i Trygg-koncernen", *Svenska Dagbladet*, 5 January 1955.
63 Letter from Elov Bergkvist, 1 June 1966. Carl Eric Almgren's archive, vol. 01:47. Swedish Military Archives.
64 Neutrality Policy Commission, "Transcript of the questioning of the former Director of Research Thede Palm", 25 February 1993, p. 23.
65 "Den fjärde försvarsgrenen", *Svenska Dagbladet*, 2 September 1953. See also Rossbach 2017.
66 On psychological warfare and resistance movements, see ch. 8 in Palm 1988.
67 Erlander 2004, 20 October 1954, p. 140.
68 Thede Palm's diary, vol. 10, 3 September 1959.

69 Gunnar Dahlander, "Det psykologiska försvarets organisation och arbetsuppgifter", no date. Board for Psychological Defence, series F II b, vol. 1. Swedish Military Archives, p. 5. See also Gunnar Heckscher, "De olika avdelningarnas huvudsakliga arbetsuppgifter vid tillämpning av kommittéförslaget", 5 November 1954. Series F II b, vol. 1. Swedish Military Archives, p. 2; "Avtal om tjänstgöring vid beredskaps- och krigstillstånd", Curt-Steffan Giesecke's personal papers 1956–1965, SAF archive, series F 6 GF. Centre for Business History.
70 Thede Palm's diary, vol. 9, 30 December 1954.
71 Thede Palm's diary, vol. 10, 7 February 1957. On the (presumed) reason for Alvar Lindencrona's anger, see 17 November 1956 in the same diary and volume.
72 Letter to Carl August Ehrensvärd, 12 March 1963. Anders Grafström's archive, vol. 5. Swedish Military Archives, p. 2.
73 Neutrality Policy Commission, "Transcript of the questioning of the former Director of Research Thede Palm", 25 February 1993, p. 23.
74 "A. Grafströms minnen", ch. 1. Anders Grafström's archive, vol. 1. Swedish Military Archives, p. 2.
75 "A. Grafströms minnen", ch. 1, pp. 7–8.
76 On the politicized view of events in Ådalen, see Svante Nycander, "Minnet är en partifråga", *Dagens Nyheter*, 30 April 2002.
77 "A. Grafströms minnen", ch. 1, pp. 8–10.
78 "A. Grafströms minnen", ch. 1, pp. 10–12. Claims that the soldiers' train was hit by shotgun fire were supported by another military eyewitness who made a statement regarding the manuscript's depiction of events in Ådalen; see letter from Nils Ankarcrona, 9 August 1979. Anders Grafström's archive, vol. 1. Swedish Military Archives.
79 "A. Grafströms minnen", ch. 1, pp. 12–13.
80 Andolf 1989, p. 51.
81 "A. Grafströms minnen", ch. 6, p. 4.
82 Kurt Andersson, "Två hundra ryssar stupa för svenska kulor", *Den Frivillige*, undated. Copy in Anders Grafström's archive, vol. 2. Swedish Military Archives.

83 "'Hjälten från Märkäjärvi' utpekas som svensk kontaktman i Haparanda", *Expressen*, 4 November 1946. Copy in Anders Grafström's archive, vol. 2. Swedish Military Archives.
84 Berggren 2022, p. 278. The Swedish units that volunteered for the Winter War also included individuals who participated for less salubrious reasons. "A couple of armed robbers and body-snatchers should have been executed by firing squad but were given a reprieve on the grounds that it was war," recalls one volunteer, who also claims that these individuals were "forcibly deprived" of their Finnish campaign medals on their way home to Sweden; see letter from Sven Hallström, 15 March 1940. Anders Grafström's archive, vol. 5. Swedish Military Archives.
85 "A. Grafströms minnen", ch. 8, p. 3.
86 "A. Grafströms minnen", ch. 8, p. 17. See also "När svenskarna hissade finska flaggan i Hangö", *Svenska Dagbladet*, 11 December 1941.
87 "Partisankrigföring", script for lectures in March and May 1944. Anders Grafström's archive, vol. 1. Swedish Military Archives.

## CHAPTER 5: OPERATION METRO

1 Thede Palm's diary, vol. 9, 8 December 1950.
2 Interview with Hans Wermdalen, 11 January 2023.
3 Mikael Holmström, interview with Curt-Steffan Giesecke, 30 July 2010. Copy in author's archive.
4 According to Høiland and Bjaaland 2024, p. 464, it would seem that "the concept *stay behind* was made famous by later media coverage". (In the quotation I have rendered *stay behind* without capitals.)
5 Fiala 2019, pp. 167–69.
6 Tamir Sinai, "Eyes on Target: 'Stay-Behind' Forces During the Cold War", *War in History* 28 (3) 2021, pp. 683–84. See also Brian Petit, "Should I Stay or Should I Go? Stay-Behind Force Decision-Making", blog post 8 November 2023. https://warontherocks.com/2023/11/should-i-stay-or-should-i-go-stay-behind-force-decision-making/
7 On free war, see Gäfvert 1994.

8 Lars-Olof Lampers, *Det grå brödraskapet: en berättelse om IB.* Report to the Security Services Commission, SOU 2002:92, p. 472. On IB during wartime, see also Ingemar Engman, "Inget samröre med Krigs-IB", *Dagens Nyheter*, 21 December 1990; Kokk 2001. On T Bureau's wartime organization, see Wikström 2006, pp. 66–67.
9 Christensen 1988, p. 26.
10 Thede Palm's diary, vol. 9, 28 December 1950.
11 Thede Palm's diary, vol. 9, 15 November 1950.
12 See, for example, "CIA/OPC Strategic War Plan in Support of the Joint Outline Emergency War Plan", 4 April 1951. https://history.state.gov/historicaldocuments/frus1950-55Intel/d61. See also Riste and Moland 1997, pp. 86–88.
13 Riste and Moland 1997, p. 88.
14 Palm 2007, p. 108. Confirmed by Høiland and Bjaaland 2024, p. 480.
15 Thede Palm's diary, vol. 9, 28 October 1949.
16 Thede Palm's diary, vol. 9, 18 November 1948.
17 Thede Palm's diary, vol. 9, 28 October 1949.
18 Thede Palm's diary, vol. 9, 13 January 1951.
19 Thede Palm's diary, vol. 9, 28 December 1950.
20 Thede Palm's diary, vol. 9, 8 December 1950.
21 Thede Palm's diary, vol. 9, 19 January 1951.
22 Thede Palm's diary, vol. 9, 20–28 January 1951. (In the quotation I have changed the punctuation.)
23 Neutrality Policy Commission, "Transcript of the questioning of General Carl Eric Almgren", 12 March 1993, p. 29. Central Archives of the Government Offices.
24 Mikael Holmström, interview with Curt-Steffan Giesecke, 31 July 2010. Copy in the author's archive.
25 Ganser and Deland 2016, p. 332.
26 Colby and Forbath 1978, pp. 82–84.
27 Thede Palm's diary, vol. 9, 8 May 1951. (In the quotation I have italicized the second sentence.)
28 Thede Palm's diary, vol. 9, 5 March 1952. In the typed diary Palm has added parentheses in pencil around the words "were involved in" and instead written in the margin: "had begun to think in terms of". This strengthens my thesis that "industrial protection" was Palm's own formulation.

29 Thede Palm's diary, vol. 9, 17 May 1952.
30 "Minutes of interrogation conducted at criminal state police station on 15 October 1952 with inventory clerk Anders Fredrik Falk." Bilaga 7 i brottsmålsakt 627/1952, p. 3. Uppsala City Court archive, G II 1:56. Uppsala County Archive. On Sveaborg fortress, see, for example, Ullman 2008.
31 See Lööw 1990, pp. 126–30.
32 Förundersökningsprotokoll. Bilaga 1 i brottsmålsakt 627/1952, pp. 7–8. Uppsala City Court archive, G II 1:56. Uppsala County Archive.
33 Förundersökningsprotokoll. Bilaga 1 i brottsmålsakt 627/1952, p. 5. Uppsala City Court archive, G II 1:56. Uppsala County Archive.
34 Förundersökningsprotokoll. Bilaga 1 i brottsmålsakt 627/1952 p. 19. Uppsala City Court archive, G II 1:56. Uppsala County Archive.
35 See Lööw 2004, pp. 361–65.
36 See appendices 1, 6, 7 and 10 i brottsmålsakt 627/1952. Uppsala City Court archive, G II 1:56. Uppsala County Archive.
37 Förundersökningsprotokoll. Bilaga 1 i brottsmålsakt 627/1952, p. 6. Uppsala City Court archive, G II 1:56. Uppsala County Archive.
38 Förundersökningsprotokoll. Bilaga 1 i brottsmålsakt 627/1952, p. 17. Uppsala City Court archive, G II 1:56. Uppsala County Archive.
39 Lööw 1990, pp. 129–30.
40 Förundersökningsprotokoll. Bilaga 1 i brottsmålsakt 627/1952, pp. 9–12. Uppsala City Court archive, G II 1:56. Uppsala County Archive.
41 "Minutes of interrogation conducted at criminal state police station with Major Anders Grafström 12 June 1952." Bilaga 2 i brottsmålsakt 627/1952, p. 30. Uppsala City Court archive, G II 1:56. Uppsala County Archive.
42 "Verdict delivered by the city court of Uppsala at the townhall on 15 April 1953." Brottmålsakt 627/1952. Uppsala City Court archive, G II 1:56. Uppsala County Archive.
43 Schön 2000, p. 399.
44 Ganser and Deland 2016, pp. 328–29. (In the quotation I have italicized *Stay behind.*)
45 Wall 2015, p. 221.

46 "Minutes of interrogation conducted at criminal state police station with Major Anders Grafström 12 June 1952." Bilaga 2 i brottsmålsakt 627/1952 ur Uppsala City Court archive, G II 1:56. Uppsala County Archive, p. 28.
47 Thede Palm's diary, vol. 9, 29 September 1952. On the "Hallberg affair", see 24 September 1952 in the same diary and volume.
48 Thede Palm's diary, vol. 9, 3 June 1952.
49 Thede Palm's diary, vol. 9, 29 October 1952.
50 Thede Palm's diary, vol. 9, 30 October 1952.
51 Thede Palm's diary, vol. 9, 29 October 1952.
52 Thede Palm's diary, vol. 9, 23 January 1954.
53 Interview with Björn von Sydow, 31 August 2023.
54 See Thede Palm's diary, vol. 9, 24 May 1954.
55 Erlander 2004, 10 June 1954, p. 88.
56 Thede Palm's diary, vol. 9, 10 June 1954. (My italics.)
57 Interview with Eric Krönmark, 9 February 2022.
58 Holmström 2011, p. 543.
59 "Angående bemyndigande för chefen för inrikesdepartementet att tillkalla en kommitté för handhavande av viss verksamhet m. m.", femtioårsprotokollet no. 14, 2 December 1955. Ministry of the Interior, Secret Archives, series A 1, vol. 2. Swedish National Archives. Released without secrecy constraints.
60 See Table A 2 in Gunnar Du Rietz, Magnus Henrekson and Daniel Waldenström, "Swedish Inheritance and Gift Taxation". IFN Working Paper no. 936, p. 26. Research Institute of Industrial Economics 2012.
61 "Angående åtgärder i anledning av granskning av vissa räkenskaper", femtioårsprotokollet no. 16, 25 October 1957. Ministry of the Interior, Secret Archives, series A 1, vol. 2. Swedish National Archives. Released without secrecy constraints.
62 "Consultation paper to fifty-year protocol 2 December 1955 shall not be preserved." Note, undated and unsigned. Ministry of the Interior, Secret Archives, series B 1, vol. 1. Swedish National Archives.
63 We can be confident of this approximate date since Thede Palm, in one of his final diary entries, on 30 June 1965 in vol. 10, describes having asked Minister of Defence Sven Andersson

to refrain from assuming control of the resistance organization: "right now it is working well [under Minister of the Interior Rune B. Johansson], and no one suspects a thing [...]."

64 Dalsjö 2006, p. 269.

## CHAPTER 6: VERTICAL CONTACT

1 Letter from "Anders" to Gösta Persson 8 October 1986. Copy in the author's archive.

2 Interview with Gösta Persson, 4 and 5 October 2022.

3 According to an advertisment, insurance company Volvia began tracking elk movements on the west coast by air at around this time; see "Volvia varnar för älg!", *Svenska Dagbladet*, 24 February 1983.

4 "Inlandsbanan – ett blodomlopp i norr", *Svenska Dagbladet*, 24 December 1980.

5 Holmström 2011, p. 396.

6 Interview with Pehr Löfgreen, 17 March 2022.

7 "Östgötabonde förlorar en halv milj[on] på torkan", *Dagens Nyheter*, 7 August 1969.

8 Conversation with Eric Krönmark, 19 October 2022.

9 Holmström 2011, p. 409.

10 Nilsson 2013, p. 26.

11 Interview with Jan Leijonhielm, 14 March 2023.

12 Fredholm 2023, p. 149.

13 Jangfeldt 2015, pp. 61–63.

14 Holmström 2011, p. 397.

15 Undated notes of interview with Reinhold Geijer. Thomas Kanger's archive, vol. 5. Swedish Labour Movement's Archives and Library, n.p. In a conversation on 19 February 2025, Thomas Kanger confirmed his own handwriting and the occasion of the interview, which he estimates took place in spring 1996.

16 TV4's investigative programme "Kalla fakta" showed the apartment, with the kind permission of its owner, Agneta Dreber, in a 1996 feature on the resistance organization. Conversation with Agneta Dreber, 29 October 2024.

17 Mikael Holmström, interview with Curt-Steffan Giesecke, 30 July 2010. Copy in author's archive.

18 Mikael Holmström, interview with Curt-Steffan Giesecke, 31 July 2010. Copy in author's archive.
19 On Trygg-Hansa's premises, see, for example, Mats Wickman, "Brutalism – ärligare än så här blir inte arkitekturen", *Svenska Dagbladet*, 31 March 2017.
20 "Småannonserna", *Dagens Nyheter*, 2 August 1977 and 23 January 1981.
21 Mikael Holmström, interview with Curt-Steffan Giesecke, 31 July 2010. Copy in author's archive.
22 Fredholm 2023, p. 153.
23 Høiland and Bjaaland 2024, p. 564.
24 A. J.'s notes, 1987. Thomas Kanger's archive, vol. 5. Swedish Labour Movement's Archives and Library, p. 4. (In the quotation I have expanded an abbreviation.)
25 Letter from Anders Grafström to A. J. 25 September 1951. Thomas Kanger's archive vol. 5. Swedish Labour Movement's Archives and Library.
26 A. J.'s notes, 1987. Thomas Kanger's archive, vol. 5. Swedish Labour Movement's Archives and Library, p. 7.
27 Thomas Kanger and Oscar Hedin, "Erlanders hemliga gerilla", *Dagens Nyheter*, 4 October 1998.
28 Letter from A. J. to unknown correspondent with illegible date in September 1953. Thomas Kanger's archive, vol. 5. Swedish Labour Movement's Archives and Library. (In the quotation I have italicized *competition area* and expanded an abbreviation.)
29 Undated notes of interview with Reinhold Geijer. Thomas Kanger's archive, vol. 5. Swedish Labour Movement's Archives and Library, n.p.
30 Letter from A. J. to unknown correspondent, 16 December 1952. Thomas Kanger's archive, vol. 5. Swedish Labour Movement's Archives and Library.
31 "Plan Maize", undated document without author. Thomas Kanger's archive, vol. 5. Swedish Labour Movement's Archives and Library.
32 See, for example, "Duties of RC", undated document. Thomas Kanger's archive, vol. 5. Swedish Labour Movement's Archives and Library.
33 Palm 1988, pp. 20–21.

34 Hardi-Kovacs 2022, p. 174.
35 Hardi-Kovacs 2022, p. 174.
36 "Dödsfall Helmer Löfgreen", *Dagens Nyheter*, 1 December 1967.
37 Undated letter from A. J. to unknown correspondent. Thomas Kanger's archive, vol. 5. Swedish Labour Movement's Archives and Library.
38 Undated notes of interview with Reinhold Geijer. Thomas Kanger's archive, vol. 5. Swedish Labour Movement's Archives and Library, n.p. (Thomas Kanger uses the same designation for Geijer's colleague from Småland as I do here.)
39 "Parad på Gärdet för 'Regi'", attributed to *Svenska Dagbladet*, 17 March 1967. Anders Grafström's archive, vol. 3. Swedish Military Archives. (In the quotation I have expanded two abbreviations.)
40 Palm 1988, p. 21.

## CHAPTER 7: *VIVAT CAROLUS REX SUECIÆ*

1 Interview with Johan Giesecke, 16 February 2023.
2 On German troop and medical transit trains, see Zetterberg 2023.
3 Seck and Åqvist 1945.
4 "Bo Balderson avslöjad?", Sveriges Radio 22 September 2009.
5 Conversation with Johan Giesecke, 23 May 2024.
6 Quoted by Jonas Fröberg in "Giesecke – en ovanlig näringslivsgigant ur tiden", *Svenska Dagbladet*, 2 February 2016.
7 Conversation with Johan Giesecke 23 May 2024.
8 Mikael Holmström, interview with Curt-Steffan Giesecke, 30 July 2010. Copy in author's archive.
9 On the Social Democrats' radicalization of labour policy in the 1970s, see, for example, Svante Nycander, "Palme sänkte den svenska modellen", *Respons* no. 1 2012.
10 Mikael Holmström, interview with Curt-Steffan Giesecke, 31 July 2010. Copy in author's archive.
11 Interview with Göran Tunhammar, 4 November 2022.
12 Robert Lugn's function in the resistance organization is mentioned in Santesson 2024, a publication financed partly

by the Swedish Armed Forces, and can therefore now be considered as being in the public domain.

13 Mikael Holmström, interview with Curt-Steffan Giesecke, 30 July 2010. Copy in author's archive.
14 Conversation with Ingemar Engman, 3 June 2022.
15 Mikael Holmström, interview with Curt-Steffan Giesecke, 10 August 2010. Copy in author's archive.
16 Conversation with Thage G. Peterson, 10 June 2024.
17 Interview with Björn Eriksson, 18 October 2022.
18 Neutrality Policy Commission, *Om kriget kommit: förberedelser för mottagande av militärt bistånd 1949–1969*, SOU 1994:11. Prime Minister's Office 1994, p. 284.
19 Interview with Michael Sahlin, 17 November 2022.
20 Mikael Holmström, "Svårt fatta försvarsbeslut även för borgerlig regering", *Svenska Dagbladet*, 13 September 1991.
21 Conversation with Peter Egardt, 14 December 2023.

## EPILOGUE

1 Stenlås 2010, p. 62.
2 Thede Palm's diary, vol. 9, 2 December 1950.
3 Jordskogen 2024, pp. 627–28. (Emphasis in original; in the quotation I have italicized *stay behind* and rendered it in lower case.)
4 Agrell 1990.
5 On the application of historical knowledge for better decision-making, see, for example, Bew, Erhardt and Hessérus 2023; Neustadt and May 1986.
6 Plokhy 2023, pp. 205–06. See also Liam Collins, Michael Kofman and John Spencer, "The Battle of Hostomel Airport: A Key Moment in Russia's Defeat in Kyiv", blog post 10 August 2023. https://warontherocks.com/2023/08/the-battle-of-hostomel-airport-a-key-moment-in-russias-defeat-in-kyiv/
7 On Ukraine's *stay-behind* groups, see Høiland and Bjaaland 2024, p. 666.
8 See Ford 2024.
9 This line of argument finds support in the Resistance Inquiry, *Kompletterande motståndsformer*, SOU 1984:10. Ministry of Defence 1984.

10 Gustafsson 2006, pp. 43–44.
11 Carlsson 2023, p. 100.
12 John Bolton, "Trump Should Lay Off NATO, Target the U.N.", *Wall Street Journal,* 8 March 2024.
13 See Karin Airaksinen, "Här är luckorna i försvaret av Sverige", *SVT Nyheter*, 14 October 2024; Ewa Stenberg and Bo Torbjörn Ek, "Upp till 1 200 svenska soldater kan skickas till Lettland nästa år", *Dagens Nyheter*, 7 October 2024; Mikael Holmström, "Svensk armétrupp på 5 000 soldater på NATO:s kravlista", *Dagens Nyheter*, 5 May 2023.
14 Karin Thurfjell, "'Vi blir säkrare men i en osäker tid'", *Svenska Dagbladet*, 29 February 2024. (In the quotation I have changed "your" to "their".)
15 Apps 2025, p. 25.
16 Agrell 2000, p. 167.
17 Therese Larsson Hultin, "Sveriges värsta scenario: 'en helt ny förmåga'", *Svenska Dagbladet*, 13 January 2025.
18 This chapter draws on the author's article "Dags att sätta fosterlandet främst" in *Fokus* no. 17 2024.
19 See, for example, James March and Johan Olsen, "Institutional Perspectives on Political Institutions", *Governance* 9 (3) 1996; "The Institutional Dynamics of International Political Orders", *International Organization* 52 (4) 1998.
20 Quoted in Kjell Goldmann, "Appropriateness and Consequences: The Logic of Neo-Institutionalism", *Governance* 18 (4) 2005, p. 46.
21 "Studio Ett", Sveriges Radio, 9 September 2024.
22 Helena Sjödin Öberg, "Nicolai ville hjälpa ambulansen ur snöstormen – men fick nej", *Dagens Nyheter*, 25 March 2024.
23 Karjel 2023, p. 75.
24 This chapter draws on the author's article "The UK and Sweden, two tales of Afghan withdrawal" in *Engelsberg Ideas*, 27 July 2025.

## AFTERWORDS

1 Schlögel 2011, p. 19. Trans. Rodney Livingstone.
2 Schlögel 2011, p. 27.
3 Agrell 2017, p. 26.

4 Palm 2007, p. 25.
5 For explanations of Thede Palm's codes for T Bureau's Western partner countries and specific personal contacts overseas, see Nilsson 2013; Andreas Ohlsson, "Synen på agentoperationerna i Baltikum genom Thede Palms dagbok 1948–1957". Swedish Defence University 2023.
6 See Caro 2019.
7 "Studio Ett", Sveriges Radio 22 December 2021.
8 See Wilhelm Agrell, "Att forska i underrättelsearkiv", *Statsvetenskaplig tidskrift* no. 3 2020.
9 See, for example, Moloney 2002.
10 Thomas Kanger and Oscar Hedin, "Erlanders hemliga gerilla", *Dagens Nyheter*, 4 October 1998.
11 Interview with Johan Giesecke, 16 February 2023.
12 "G[iesecke]'s wife and children were not aware and G[iesecke] never travelled with a 'cover'. He was well aware that he would be in personal danger if the situation became acute." Elisabeth Lindencrona Paues's and Staffan Paues's interview notes from a meeting with Curt-Steffan Giesecke, 26 November 2013, p. 1. Copy in the author's archive.
13 Interview with Elisabeth Lindencrona Paues, 6 January 2022.
14 See, for example, "Alla vi som älskar våra barn", *Husmodern* no. 38 1949; "Äntligen blev det av", *Idun* no. 39 1949.
15 Conversation with Elisabeth Lindencrona Paues, 19 May 2022.
16 Interview with Elisabeth Lindencrona Paues, 6 January 2022.
17 Conversation with Elisabeth Lindencrona Paues, 21 October 2024.
18 Interview with Elisabeth Lindencrona Paues, 6 January 2022.
19 Conversation with Elisabeth Lindencrona Paues, 21 October 2024.
20 Interview with Elisabeth Lindencrona Paues, 6 January 2022. Conversation, 17 January 2024.
21 Conversation with Elisabeth Lindencrona Paues, 13 March 2025.
22 Conversation with Elisabeth Lindencrona Paues, 19 May 2022.
23 Bjarne Stenquist, "Sovjet visste allt om gruppen", *Dagens Nyheter*, 15 August 1991.
24 Letter from Alvar Lindencrona, 5 January 1964, p. 2. Copy in the author's archive.

25 Conversation with Elisabeth Lindencrona Paues, 21 October 2024.
26 "Fel man utpekad", *Dagens Nyheter*, 21 August 1991. (In the quotation I have expanded an abbreviation.)
27 Thede Palm, "PM ang[ående] Donald Prater", 12 May 1970, p. 1. Thede Palm's diary, vol. 10.
28 Thede Palm, "PM ang[ående] Donald Prater", 12 May 1970, p. 2. Thede Palm's diary, vol. 10.
29 Conversation with Nigel West, 21 February 2024.
30 The Venona traffic is now freely accessible on the homepage for the United States' signals intelligence service NSA. https://www.nsa.gov/Helpful-Links/NSA-FOIA/Declassification-Transparency-Initiatives/Historical-Releases/Venona/
31 Thede Palm, "PM ang[ående] Donald Prater", 12 May 1970, p. 2. Thede Palm's diary, vol. 10.

# Sources and Bibliography

## ORAL SOURCES


Fredrik von Arnold: interview 17 January 2023.
Carl Banér: conversation 11 January 2024; conversation 30 September 2024.
Bengt: interview 16 February 2022.
Ingvar Carlsson: interview 24 November 2021.
Curt: conversation 25 January 2022; conversation 25 September 2023.
Agneta Dreber: conversation 29 October 2024.
Peter Egardt: conversation 14 December 2023.
Ingemar Engman: interview 4 March 2022.
Björn Eriksson: interview 18 October 2022.
Johan Giesecke: interview 16 February 2023; conversation 23 May 2024.
Ole Grøn: conversation 30 March 2022.
Jan Guillou: conversation 26 March 2024.
Lars-Olov Johansson: conversation 7 May 2024.
Bertil Jonsson: interview 3 October 2022.
Hanna Jungwallius: conversation 20 March 2024.
Thomas Kanger: conversation 19 February 2025.
Carl Kleman: interview 22 November 2023; conversation 29 November 2023; conversation 26 September 2024; conversation 11 October 2024.
Eric Krönmark: interview 9 February 2022; conversation 19 October 2022.

Jan Leijonhielm: interview 14 March 2023.
Elisabeth Lindencrona Paues: interview 6 January 2022; conversation 19 May 2022; conversation 11 September 2023; interview 17 January 2024; conversation 21 October 2024; conversation 13 March 2025.
Gustaf Lindencrona: interview 27 October 2021.
Pehr Löfgreen: interview 17 March 2022.
Svante Nycander: interview 23 January 2023.
Olof: conversation 25 September 2024.
Ebba Palm-Lamoureux: interview 16 November 2022.
Gösta Persson: interview 4 and 5 October 2022.
Thage G. Peterson: conversation 10 June 2024.
Ingrid Rosander: interview 11 January 2022.
Michael Sahlin: interview 17 November 2022.
Björn von Sydow: interview 14 December 2021; interview 19 April 2023; interview 31 August 2023.
Göran Tunhammar: interview 4 November 2022.
Evabritta Wallberg: interview 10 January 2023.
Hans Wermdalen: interview 11 January 2023.
Nigel West: conversation 21 February 2024.

## UNPUBLISHED SOURCES AND ARTEFACTS

(Details of records, series and volumes are given only in the Notes.)

*Privately owned*

Johan Giesecke (Södertälje)
Glass originally owned by Curt-Steffan Giesecke, inscribed *Vivat Carolus Rex Suecia*
Mikael Holmström (Sollentuna)
Transcribed interviews with Curt-Steffan Giesecke 30 and 31 July and 10 August 2010
Elisabeth Lindencrona Paues (Stockholm)
Letter from Alvar Lindencrona 5 January 1964
Interview notes from meeting with Curt-Steffan Giesecke 26 November 2013
Undated noted from Lennart Grundborn
Gustaf Lindencrona (Stockholm)

Alvar Lindencrona's pocket calendar 1948–67 (incomplete series)
Gösta Persson (Östersund)
Letter from "Anders" 8 October 1986
Letter from "Anders" 16 June 1987
Note from "Anders" 2 June 1988

*Swedish Labour Movement's Archives and Library, Huddinge*
Tage Erlander's archive
Arne Geijer's archive
Thomas Kanger's archive
Olof Palme's archive

*Centre for Business History, Bromma*
Curt-Steffan Giesecke's records, Swedish Employers' Federation archive
Bertil Kugelberg's records, Swedish Employers' Federation archive

*Uppsala County Archive*
Uppsala City Court archive

*Central Archives of the Government Offices, Stockholm*
Neutrality Policy Commission archive
Security Policy Inquiry archive

*Swedish National Archives, Arninge (Military Archives)*
Board for Psychological Defence
Carlos Adlercreutz's archive
Carl Eric Almgren's archive
Defence Staff C Bureau
Anders Grafström's archive
Helge Jung's archive
Thede Palm's archive
Nils Swedlund's archive

*Swedish National Archives, Marieberg*
Alvar Lindencrona's archive
Ministry of the Interior's Secret Archives
Security Services Commission's Archives

## PUBLISHED SOURCES AND BIBLIOGRAPHY

(Details of research, news and other articles as well as conference presentations, reports, commissions of inquiry and the like are given only in the Notes.)

Agrell, Wilhelm, *Det välorganiserade nederlaget* (Ordfront, 1990)

Agrell, Wilhelm, *Fred och fruktan: Sveriges säkerhetspolitiska historia 1918–2000* (Historiska Media, 2000)

Agrell, Wilhelm, *Sprickor i järnridån: svensk underrättelsetjänst 1944–1992* (Historiska Media, 2017)

Andolf, Göran, "Svenska Frivilligkåren", in Stig Claëson, Stig Löwgren, Gunnar Nordlöf and Mascoll Silfverstolpe (eds), *Svenska frivilliga i Finland 1939–1944* (Militärhistoriska Förlaget, 1989)

Andræ, Tor m.fl., *I angeläget ärende* (Albert Bonniers Förlag, 1941)

Andreen, Per G., Arvid Fredborg, Torvald T:son Höjer, Th. Åke Leissner, Per Gunnar Nordin and Gunnar Unger, *Den svenska linjen* (I. Hæggströms Boktryckeri, 1940)

Apps, Peter, *Deterring Armageddon: A Biography of NATO* (Wildfire, 2025)

Bergelin, Eric, *Planeringsforskningens genombrott: Försvarets forskningsanstalt och det kalla krigets planeringsexperter* (Acta Universitatis Upsaliensis, 2023)

Berggren, Henrik, *Underbara dagar framför oss: en biografi över Olof Palme* (Norstedts, 2010)

Berggren, Henrik, *Landet utanför: Sverige och kriget 1940–1942* (Norstedts, 2022)

Berggren, Henrik, *Landet utanför: Sverige och kriget 1943–1945* (Norstedts, 2023)

Bergstrand, Mats, *Framför lyckta dörrar: en bok om Anders Björck* (Jure, 2002)

Bew, John, Andrew Erhardt and Mattias Hessérus (eds), *Tillämpad historia: klassiska texter* (Bokförlaget Stolpe, 2023)

Blaadh, Walther, *Sovjetisk invasion av Sverige: hur planerade Sovjet att invadera Sverige? Vad visste de? Hemliga kartor, planer och förband* (Svenskt Militärhistoriskt Biblioteks Förlag, 2025)

Bokholm, Rune, *Tisdagsklubben: om glömda antinazistiska sanningssägare i svenskt 30- och 40-tal* (Atlantis, 2001) von Braun, Joakim and Lars Gyllenhaal, *Ryska elitförband: spetsnaz, osnaz, VDV och andra elitstyrkor* (Fischer & Co, 2013)

Carlsson, Staffan, *Helgon och maktspelare: Dag Hammarskjöld som politiker* (Albert Bonniers Förlag, 2023)

Caro, Robert A., *Working: Researching, Interviewing, Writing* (Alfred A. Knopf, 2019)

Christensen, Christian, *Vår hemmelige beredskap: historien om MM* (Cappelen, 1988)

Civilförsvarsstyrelsen, *Om kriget kommer* (1961)

Colby, William and Peter Forbath, *Honorable Men: My Life in the CIA* (Simon & Schuster, 1978)

Dalsjö, Robert, *Life-Line Lost: The Rise and Fall of "Neutral" Sweden's Secret Reserve Option of Wartime Help from the West* (Santérus Academic Press, 2006)

De Geer, Lars-Erik, *Kärnvapen på svensk mark! … om avslöjandet av kärnvapen ombord på sovjetiska ubåten U-137* (Ranunkel förlag, 2024)

Dobbs, Michael, *One Minute to Midnight: Kennedy, Khrushchev and Castro on the Brink of Nuclear War* (Hutchinson, 2008)

Ehrensvärd, Carl August, *Hårt mot hårt: blixtanfall och blixtförsvar* (Norstedts, 1943)

Ehrensvärd, Carl August, *Arméchef i orostid: dagboksanteckningar 1938–1957* (Svenskt Militärhistoriskt Bibliotek, 2005)

Erlander, Tage, *1901–1939* (Tiden, 1972)

Erlander, Tage, *Dagböcker 1945–1949* (Gidlunds, 2001a)

Erlander, Tage, *Dagböcker 1950–1951* (Gidlunds, 2001b)

Erlander, Tage, *Dagböcker 1954* (Gidlunds, 2004)

Fiala, Otto C. (ed.), *Resistance Operating Concept* (Försvarshögskolan, 2019)

Ford, Matthew, "War in the Age of the Smartphone: Ukraine and Contemporary Conflict", in Matthew Hefler (ed.), *Intelligence and Contemporary Conflict: Communication in Diplomacy, Statecraft and War* (Bokförlaget Stolpe, 2024)

Forsberg, Tuomas and Magnus Christiansson, *NATO's Northern Enlargement: Finland and Sweden's Path to Membership* (Bristol University Press, 2025)

Försvarsdepartementet, *Totalförsvarets författningshandbok 2021/22* (Norstedts Juridik, 2021)

Fredborg, Lars, *Jag måste ha varit olidlig: Arvid Fredborg, krigskorrespondent, författare och rådgivare* (Ekerlids Förlag, 2023)
Fredholm, Michael, *Hemligstämplat: svensk underrättelsetjänst från Erlander till Bildt* (Medströms Bokförlag, 2021)
Fredholm, Michael, "Dolda bakom olika täcknamn: IB:s utrikes- och inrikesunderrättelsetjänst", in Wilhelm Agrell et al., *Guide till spionernas och underrättelsetjänsternas Sverige* (Medströms Bokförlag, 2023)
Gäfvert, Björn, "Det fria kriget: från idé till krigsorganisation", in Bo Hugemark Bo (ed.), *Nya fronter? 1943 – spänd väntan* (Probus, 1994)
Ganser, Daniele and Mats Deland, "Det hemliga kriget i Sverige", in Daniele Ganser, *NATO:s hemliga arméer: operation Gladio och terrorismen i Västeuropa* (Karneval, 2016)
Gilmour, John, *Sweden, the Swastika and Stalin: The Swedish Experience in the Second World War* (Edinburgh University Press, 2010)
Grøn, Ole, "'Onkler', 'tanter' og et hemmeligt netværk", in Peter la Cour (ed.), *Stay Behind. Hemmeligt netværk i Danmark* (Peter la Cours Forlag, 2018)
Grundborn, Lennart, *Havet vi ärvde: Grundsund i tidens hav* (Båtdokgruppen, 2012)
Grundborn, Lennart, *Sista dansen med Thule* (Lennart Grundborn, 2006)
Gustafsson, Bengt, *Det "kalla kriget": några reflexioner* (Försvarshögskolan, 2006)
Gustafsson, Bengt, *Det sovjetiska hotet mot Sverige under det kalla kriget* (Försvarshögskolan, 2007)
Hansson, Per Albin, "Svensk folkpolitik", in Per Albin Hansson, *Demokrati: tal och uppsatser* (Tiden, 1935)
Hardi-Kovacs, Gellert, *C-byrån hemligast av alla: berättelsen om Sveriges hemliga underrättelse under andra världskriget* (Carlssons, 2022)
von Heidenstam, Verner, *Karolinerna* (Albert Bonniers Förlag, 1914)
Hjort, Magnus, *Folk och Försvar och kampen mot den femte kolonnen: en studie i framväxten av Övervaknings-Sverige under 1950-talet* (Stockholms universitet and Södertörns högskola, 1998)
Hjulström, Anders, "Milo Ö – vitalt och komplicerat", in Bo Hugemark (ed.), *Den stora invasionen* (Medströms Bokförlag, 2017)

Høiland, Geir Arild and Torstein Bjaaland, *Stay behind: forsvarets hemmelige avdelning 1946–1990, bind 1: bakgrunn, oppbygging, beredskap* (Pax Forlag, 2023)

Høiland, Geir Arild and Torstein Bjaaland, *Stay behind: forsvarets hemmelige avdelning 1946–1990, bind 2: på innsiden av Stay behind* (Pax Forlag, 2024)

Holmström, Mikael, *Den dolda alliansen: Sveriges hemliga NATO-förbindelser* (Atlantis, 2011)

Hugemark, Bo, "På vakt: beredskap mot överraskande angrepp och kränkningar", in Bo Hugemark (ed.), *Försvaret och kalla kriget: krigsavhållande försvar* (Medströms Bokförlag, 2024)

Husén, Torsten, *Psykologisk krigföring* (Gleerups, 1942)

Jackson, Walter A., *Gunnar Myrdal and America's Conscience: Social Engineering and Radical Liberalism, 1938–1987* (University of North Carolina Press, 1990)

Jangfeldt, Bengt, *Med livet som insats: berättelsen om Vladimir Majakovskij och hans krets* (Wahlström & Widstrand, 2007)

Jangfeldt, Bengt, *Raoul Wallenberg: en biografi* (Wahlström & Widstrand, 2012)

Jangfeldt, Bengt, *En rysk historia* (Wahlström & Widstrand, 2015)

Jansson, Nils-Ove, *Omöjlig ubåt: stridsberättelser från ubåtsjakten och det säkerhetspolitiska läget under 1980-talet* (Nils-Ove Jansson, 2014)

Jansson, Nils-Ove, *Ryska ubåtsoperationer mot Sverige och i Norden* (Nils-Ove Jansson, 2023)

Jensen, Frank, *Min far var spion* (People's Press, 2019)

Johansson, Anders L., *Rikshushållaren: Gunnar Sträng i socialdemokratins tjänst 1906–1992* (Atlas, 2018)

Jordskogen, Odd Bjørn, "Internasjonal lov", in Geir Arild Høiland and Torstein Bjaaland, *Stay behind: forsvarets hemmelige avdelning 1946–1990, bind 2: på innsiden av Stay behind* (Pax Forlag, 2024)

Karjel, Robert, *Ut ur Kabul: den svenska evakueringen från Afghanistan* (Bazar Förlag, 2023)

Kassman, Charles, *Arne Geijer och hans tid: 1910–1956* (Tiden, 1989)

Kokk, Enn, *Vitbok: militärens hemliga nätverk i arbetarrörelsen* (Hjalmarson & Högberg, 2001)

Kugelberg, Bertil, *Upp i vind* (Norstedts, 1985)

Kugelberg, Bertil, *Från en central utsiktspunkt* (Norstedts, 1986)

Le Carré, John, *Tinker Tailor Soldier Spy* (Sceptre 1999 [1974])
Lewin, Leif, *Planhushållningsdebatten* (Almqvist & Wiksell, 1967)
Lindbeck, Assar, *Ekonomi är att välja: memoarer* (Bonnier, 2012)
Lööw, Heléne, *Hakkorset och Wasakärven: en studie av nationalsocialismen i Sverige 1924–1950* (Göteborgs universitet, 1990)
Lööw, Heléne, *Nazismen i Sverige 1924–1979: pionjärerna, partierna, propagandan* (Ordfront, 2004)
Moloney, Ed, *A Secret History of the IRA* (Allen Lane, 2002)
Neustadt, Richard E. and Ernest R. May, *Thinking in Time: The Uses of History for Decision Makers* (Free Press, 1986)
Nilsson, Sam, *T-kontoret: underrättelsetjänst och västsamarbete* (Medströms Bokförlag, 2013)
Osterman, Stig, *Satt och osatt: fyra decennier i och runt Jordbrukarnas Föreningsblad* (Land, 1973)
Palm, Thede, *Wendische Kultstätten: quellenkritische Untersuchungen zu den letzten Jahrhunderten slavischen Heidentums* (Gleerupska universitetsbokhandeln, 1937)
Palm, Thede, "Uppsalalunden och Uppsalatemplet", in *Årsbok* (Vetenskapssocieteten i Lund, 1942)
Palm, Thede, *Trädkult* (Gleerup, 1948)
Palm, Thede, *Motstånd och motståndsrörelser* (Militärhistoriska Förlaget, 1988)
Palm, Thede, *T-kontoret: några studier till T-kontorets historia* [2. edition]; edited by Evabritta Wallberg (Kungl. Samfundet för utgivande av handskrifter rörande Skandinaviens historia, 2007)
Persson, Carl, *Utan omsvep* (Norstedts, 1990)
Petraeus, David and Andrew Roberts, *Conflict: The Evolution of Warfare from 1945 to Ukraine* (HarperCollins, 2023)
Plokhy, Serhii, *Det rysk-ukrainska kriget: historiens återkomst* (Albert Bonniers Förlag, 2023)
Riste, Olav and Arnfinn Moland, *"Strengt hemmelig": norsk etterretningsteneste 1945–1970* (Universitetsforlaget, 1997)
Rosell, Carl Magnus, "Thulehuset – det första 'vetenskapliga' kontorshuset", in Carl Magnus Rosell, *Kvarteret Träsket: från snus till försäkring* (Skandia, 1981)
Rossbach, Niklas, *Fighting Propaganda: The Swedish Experience of Psychological Warfare and Sweden's Psychological Defence,*

*1940–1960* (Axel och Margaret Ax:son Johnsons stiftelse för allmännyttiga ändamål, 2017)
Rothstein, Bo, *Den korporativa staten: intresseorganisationer och statsförvaltning i svensk politik* (Norstedts Juridik, 1992)
Rudberg, Erik (ed.), *Svenska Dagbladets årsbok: tjugosjätte årgången (händelserna 1948)* (Gummessons Boktryckeri, 1949)
Ruin, Olof, *I välfärdsstatens tjänst: Tage Erlander 1946–1949* (Tiden, 1986)
Santesson, Olof, "Kalla kriget – lexikon", in Bo Hugemark (ed.), *Försvaret och kalla kriget: krigsavhållande försvar* (Medströms Bokförlag, 2024)
Sarotte, M. E., *Not One Inch: America, Russia, and the Making of the Post-Cold War Stalemate* (Yale University Press, 2021)
Schlögel, Karl, *Terror och dröm: Moskva år 1937* (Natur och Kultur, 2011)
Schön, Bosse, *Svenskarna som stred för Hitler: ett historiskt reportage* (Månpocket, 2000)
Seck, Ture and Rune Åqvist, *All världens limerickar: en antologi* (Limerickförlaget, 1945)
Security Policy Inquiry, *Fred och säkerhet* (Fritzes, 2002)
Stenlås, Niklas, "Military Technology, National Identity and the State: The Rise and Decline of a Small State's Military-Industrial Complex", in Per Lundin, Niklas Stenlås and Johan Gribble (eds), *Science for Welfare and Warfare: Technology and State Initiative in Cold War Sweden* (Science History Publications/ USA, 2010)
Swenson, Peter A., *Capitalists Against Markets: The Making of Labor Markets and Welfare States in the United States and Sweden* (Oxford University Press, 2002)
Torstendahl, Rolf, *Mellan nykonservatism och liberalism: idébrytningar inom högern och bondepartierna 1918–1934* (Svenska bokförlaget, 1969)
Tynander, Thomas, *Allan Mann: svensken som stred mot Hitler och Stalin* (Bazar Förlag, 2023)
Ullman, Magnus, *Sjöfästningen Sveaborgs fall 1808: förräderi eller krigslist* (Magnus Ullman, 2008)
Vinge, P. G., *Säpochef 1962–70* (Wahlström & Widstrand, 1988)
Wall, Gunnar, *Konspiration Olof Palme: mordet, politikern och hans tysta fiender* (Semic, 2015)

Westerberg, Rikard, *Socialists at the Gate: Swedish Business and the Defense of Free Enterprise, 1940–1985* (Handelshögskolan, 2020)

Wikström, Niklas, *Den svenska militära underrättelsetjänsten 1948–1956* (Försvarshögskolan, 2006)

Winter, Harry, *Operation Garbo: en thriller om en möjlig verklighet* (Timbro, 1988)

Zetterberg, Kent, "Stay-behind i Sverige", in Anders Frankson (ed.), *Sverige under kalla kriget: myter och legender* (Lind & Co, 2021a)

Zetterberg, Kent, *Sverige och Hitler 1939–1945: ett bidrag till historien om Sverige och Tyskland under andra världskriget* (Carlssons, 2021b)

Zetterberg, Kent, *Tyskar på tåg: Sverige och beredskapen 1939–1945* (Svenskt Militärhistoriskt Biblioteks Förlag, 2023)

Zubok, Vladislav and Constantine Pleshakov, *Inside the Kremlin's Cold War: From Stalin to Khrushchev* (Harvard University Press, 1996)

# Index